CUTENESS, CONSERVATISM, AND CONSUMPTION

CUTENESS, CONSERVATISM, AND CONSUMPTION

LEFOR-OPENO AND POSTWAR FRANCE

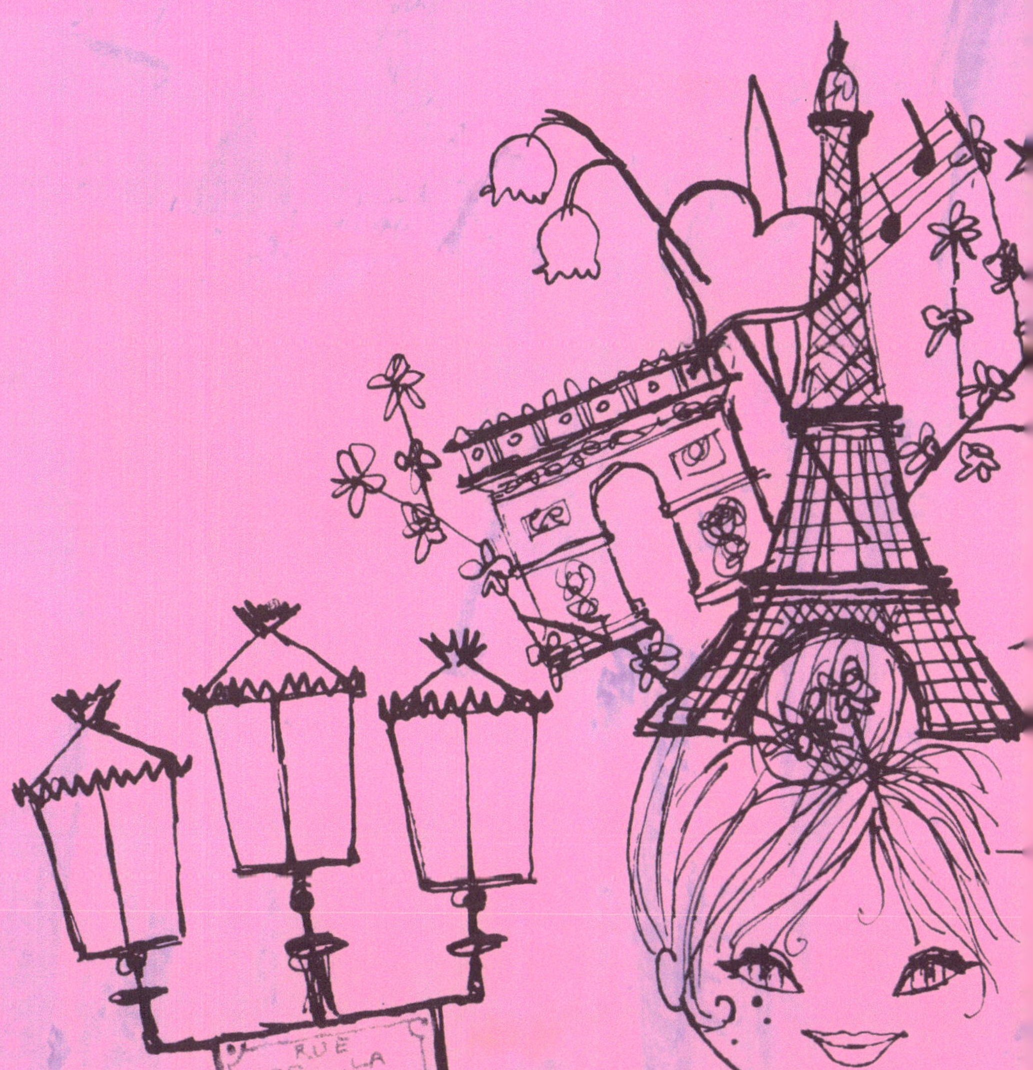

ANGELINA LIPPERT
WITH **MICHAEL LELLOUCHE**
AND **VINCENT JOIGNEAUX**

RIT PRESS
ROCHESTER, NEW YORK

Published and distributed by:
RIT Press
90 Lomb Memorial Drive
Rochester, New York 14623
https://press.rit.edu

Printed in the United States of America

ISBN 978-1-956313-59-8 (print)
ISBN 978-1-956313-60-4 (electronic)

Library of Congress Cataloging-in-Publication Data

Names: Lippert, Angelina author
Title: Cuteness, conservatism, and consumption : Lefor-Openo and postwar France / edited by Angelina Lippert ; with Michael Lellouche and Vincent Joigneaux.
Description: Rochester, New York : RIT Press, [2026]
Identifiers: LCCN 2026020906 (print) | LCCN 2026020907 (ebook) | ISBN 9781956313598 paperback | ISBN 9781956313604 ebook
Subjects: LCSH: Lefor-Openo | Art and society—France—History—20th century | LCGFT: Exhibition catalogs | Posters
Classification: LCC NC1850.L39 A4 2026 (print) | LCC NC1850.L39 (ebook)
LC record available at https://lccn.loc.gov/2026020906
LC ebook record available at https://lccn.loc.gov/2026020907

We gather on the traditional territory of the Onöndowa'ga:' or "the people of the Great Hill." In English, they are known as Seneca people, "the keeper of the western door." They are one of the six nations that make up the sovereign Haudenosaunee Confederacy.

We honor the land on which RIT was built and recognize the unique relationship that the Indigenous stewards have with this land. That relationship is the core of their traditions, cultures, and histories. We recognize the history of genocide, colonization, and assimilation of Indigenous people that took place on this land. Mindful of these histories, we work towards understanding, acknowledging, and ultimately reconciliation.

Cover: Detail of *Vichy*, c. 1958. See page 97 for full image.
Designed by Marnie Soom

CONTENTS

FOREWORD

When I joined Poster House as its inaugural curator in 2017, one of the goals the director and I agreed on was ensuring that the museum celebrated classic poster history while also working to expand the canon. Since then, we have hosted numerous exhibitions focusing on lesser-known figures in graphic design history, predominantly women. I am so pleased that a retrospective on Marie-Claire Lefort and Marie-Francine Oppeneau (together known as Lefor-Openo) has now joined that roster.

For many decades, Lefor-Openo's posters have been dismissed as too cutesy or uniform in style to be taken seriously by poster historians. This book and the accompanying exhibition, however, reveal that their graphic sensibility reflected a larger cultural shift within postwar France—projecting not only how the country wanted the world to see it, but also how it wanted to see itself. Optimism, cheeky wit, and youthful vibrancy dominated the streets, ushering France into the height of the Charles de Gaulle years and the economic prosperity that ensued.

Lefor-Openo's posters are not just whimsical calls to consumerism, but documents of major social, political, and economic events that happened in rapid succession from the 1950s through the 1970s in France. Their work chronicles the rise of de Gaulle, the Algerian War, the introduction of a key pillar to the French welfare system, the need to rebrand the city of Vichy in the wake of the World War II Nazi Occupation , the rise of the French middle class, the role of women and their ability to vote, the nationalization of French industry, the recalibration of the franc, the modernization of the domestic sphere, and various public-health initiatives that helped better the lives of countless French citizens. In short, their posters serve as a window into the complex and nuanced dynamics of French life for 20 incredibly important years.

While there exists little information on these two artists in general, I am beyond thrilled that we are able to publish the first book in English about Lefor-Openo. I invite future scholars to use this as a jumping-off point for further research and exploration into their oeuvre, and I hope all audiences are as delighted as I've been in becoming acquainted with their beautiful, historically rich contributions to graphic design history.

Angelina Lippert
Executive Director and Curator
Poster House

CUTENESS, CONSERVATISM, AND CONSUMPTION

LEFOR-OPENO AND POSTWAR FRANCE

In the aftermath of World War II, France faced a daunting recovery challenge. A significant portion of the country's young male population was either dead, wounded, or held in prisoner-of-war camps; its industry was in tatters; its farms (and therefore its ability to produce food) were decimated; and its citizens were demoralized by the collaboration of the Vichy government with the Nazis. The French economy had also halved in size since before the war and was further threatened by rampant inflation and shortages, leaving most people unable to purchase much beyond basic necessities.

The next two decades would be defined by rapid demographic and economic growth, as well as the significant social and political changes primarily brought about by General Charles de Gaulle after he was coaxed out of retirement in 1958 (first as appointed prime minister, then as elected president). His vision to rebuild France as an independent global power impacted every part of French life, from its economy to its shopping habits, its moral codes to its leisure pursuits. The posters produced during this period, however, rarely hinted at this turbulent landscape. Instead, advertising focused on bright, optimistic images that saturated the streets with cute rather than with chaos. Along with the work of major male artists like Raymond Savignac and Hervé Morvan, many of these extreme changes were also chronicled, indirectly, in the posters produced by a new female design team known as Lefor-Openo.

Marie-Claire Lefort and Marie-Francine Oppeneau came of age as France was searching for a new postwar identity. They met at the Lycée Claude Bernard in Paris, where they were studying drawing with the goal of becoming teachers. They soon realized, however, that they preferred making art to instructing students and that they wanted to work together on projects. They enrolled at the École Paul Colin, an art and design school founded in 1930 by Colin, one of the most successful and famous French poster designers of the 20th century. At a time when there were few other notable women in that profession in the country, Colin himself pushed them away from their original interest in theatrical set design toward the medium that had made him famous. Working collaboratively, the two women sought a simpler and catchier version of their long names with which to sign their posters. They ultimately embraced "Lefor-Openo" as their moniker—a choice that would stick with them throughout their 12-year career as poster designers.

WOMEN IN MALE FIELDS

In 1950s France, there were very few noteworthy female poster designers. Unlike many other Northern European countries that were getting used to the idea of women having careers, societal expectations in France dictated that a woman's duty was to be a wife and a mother. Women only obtained the right to vote in 1944, and while that legislation passed with a clear majority, many still argued that allowing women that voice would turn the country away from its traditional values. In 1955, the state expanded the availability of social benefits, including a financial stipend for stay-at-home mothers regardless of the husband's income, emphasizing its desire for women to remain out of the workforce. Women who did work were most often widows or single mothers who did so out of necessity and were typically employed in factory and domestic jobs with no hope for advancement. Professional careers were highly unusual for women and were almost always held by those from upper-middle-class backgrounds. Marie-Claire Lefort and Marie-Francine Oppeneau fit this model, enabling them to enter an otherwise male field.

Despite their socioeconomic advantages, their careers in poster design would not have taken off without the assistance of certain family connections. Marie-Claire Lefort's father was an architect who also worked for the city of Vichy, and through his influence they gained access to a handful of early design opportunities for events in the municipality and other government-sponsored initiatives. Lefor-Openo's big break, however, occurred in 1955 when they were both just 24 years old. They submitted a poster design for the Concours Lépine, an annual exposition of new French inventions. Their illustration of a man observing a flower made out of gears won the commission, bringing their work to a large audience. Their posters from this period reflect Lefor-Openo's early artistic development, showing that they first imitated popular graphic styles of the era before embracing the more upbeat, cartoonish characters that would become their signature by the late 1950s and that would reflect the general mood of postwar France.

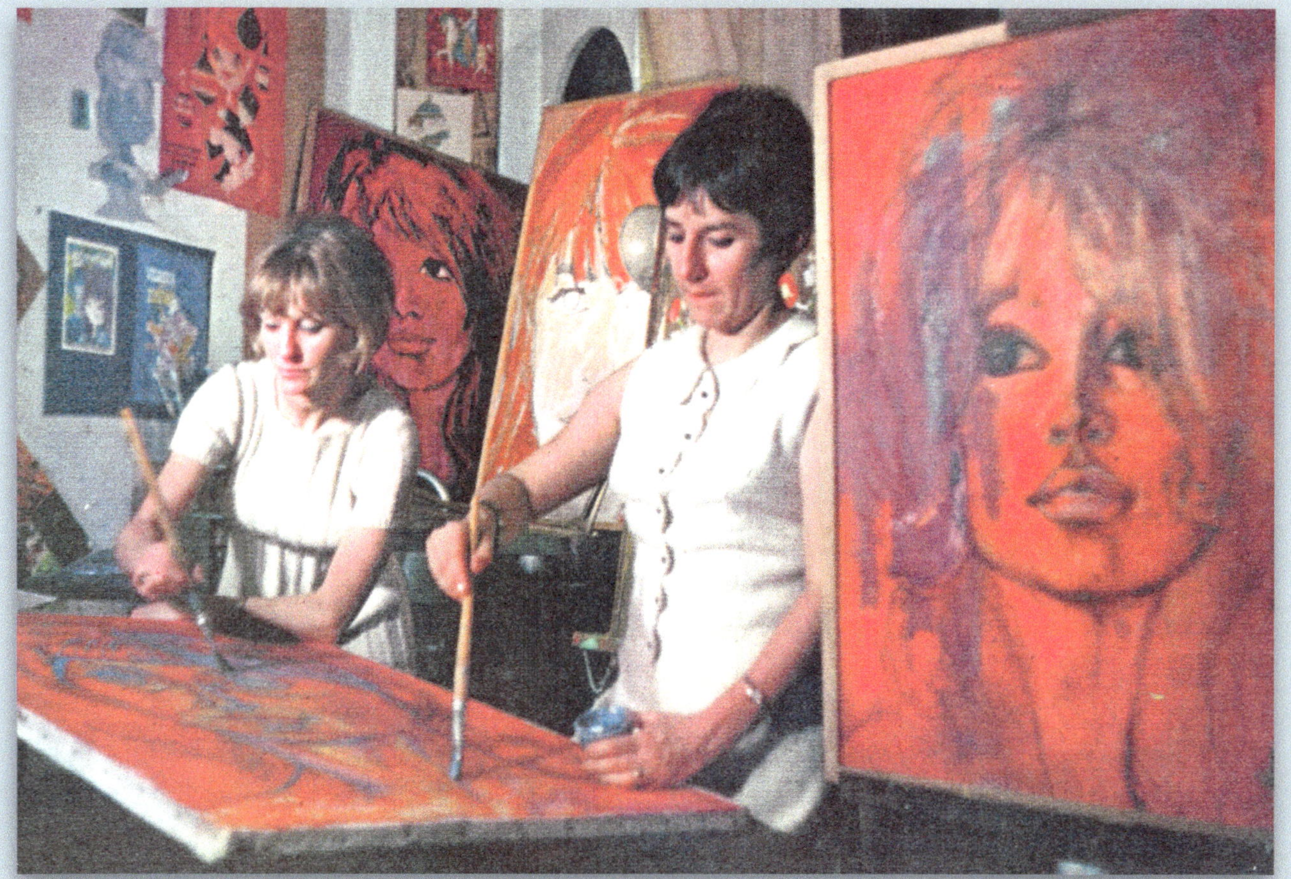

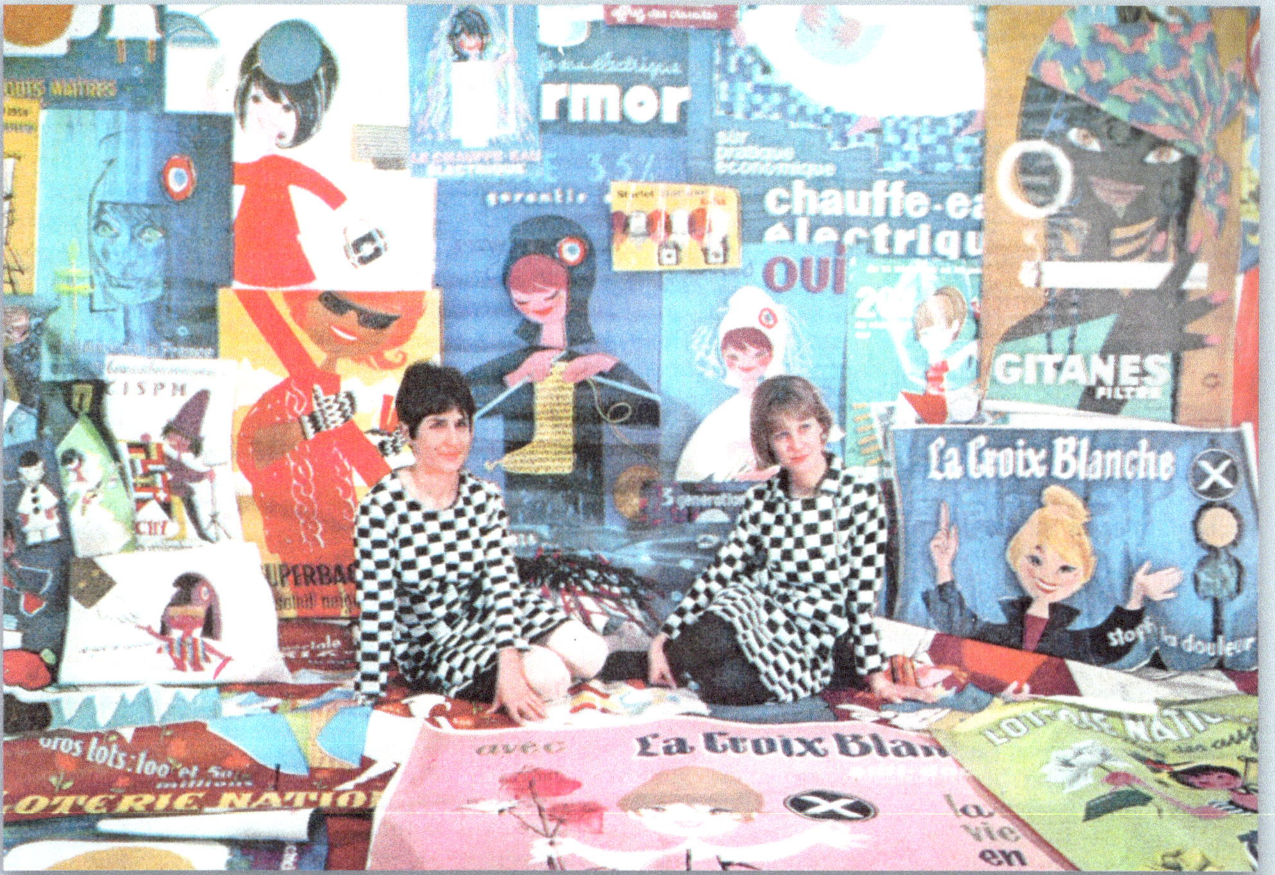

rmor
chauffe-ea
électriqu
oui
GITANES
La Croix Blanche
La Croix Blan
LOTERIE NATIO
gros lots: 100 et 5
SUPERBA
CISPM

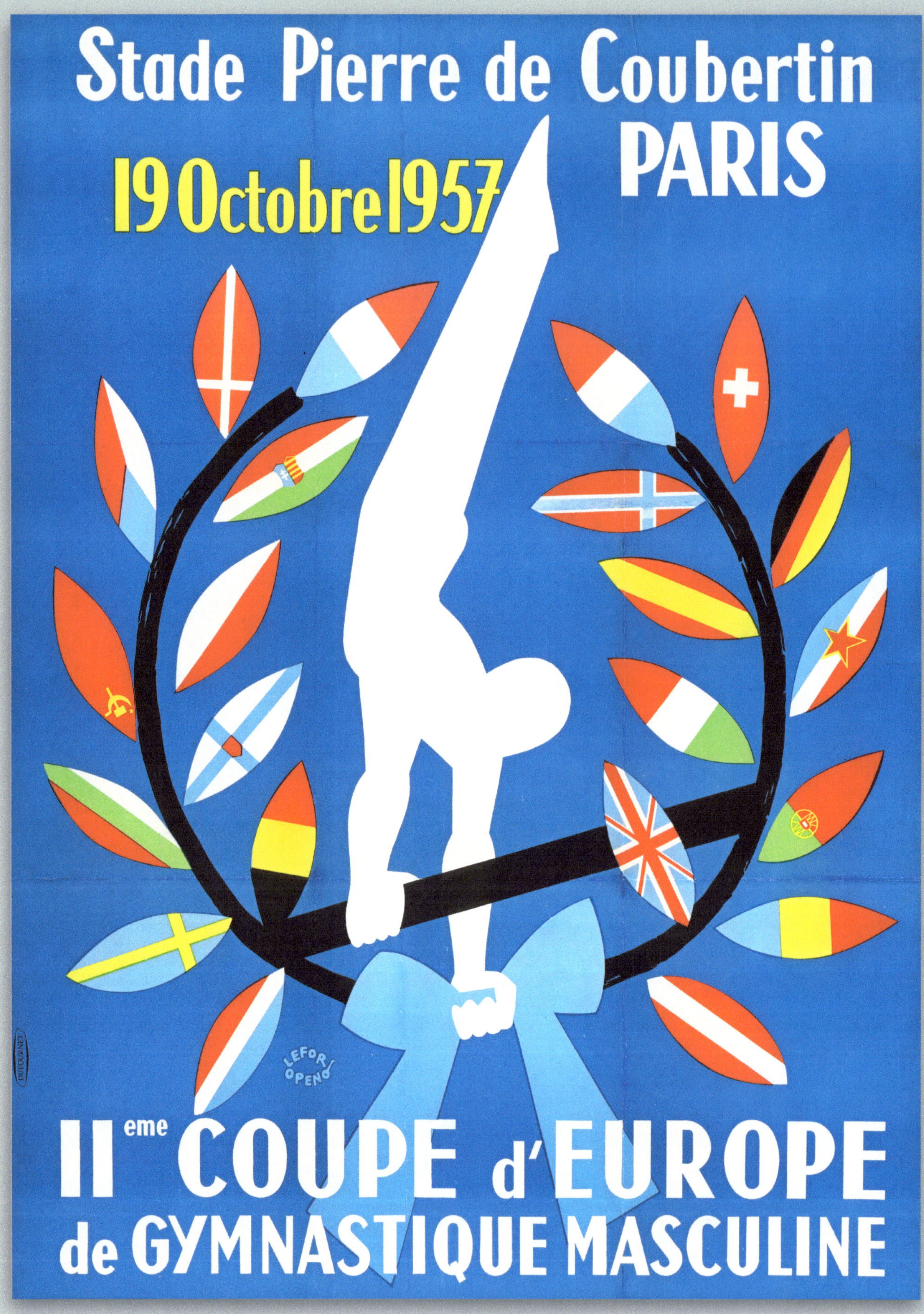

Stade Pierre de Coubertin
PARIS
19 Octobre 1957
LEFOR OPENO
IIeme COUPE d'EUROPE
de GYMNASTIQUE MASCULINE

IIeme Coupe d'Europe, 1957

Lefor-Openo (Marie-Claire Lefort, 1931–1971, and Marie-Francine Oppeneau, 1931–2023)

Poster House Permanent Collection

- After winning the poster competition to promote the Concours Lépine in 1955, Lefor-Openo received a few noteworthy commissions for other Parisian events, including this design for the Second European Men's Artistic Gymnastics Championship.
- The image is representative of most generic poster designs of the period, with simple, sans-serif text (sharp typography without flourishes) and a nondescript composition that could advertise any number of sporting events. It bears very little resemblance to the style for which Lefor-Openo would become known within a year and was most likely produced with strong direction from the sponsoring organization, allowing the designers little room for creativity.
- Hosting international events like this was very important for France's self-image in the postwar period, as it was eager to maintain its prewar reputation as the cultural capital of the world.
- In 1949, Germany was officially divided into two countries, but they shared the same national flag during sporting events (including the Olympic Games). This would change in 1959 when the German Democratic Republic (East Germany) added a hammer and compass surrounded by rye to the center of the design. In this poster, the unified German flag fills the second laurel leaf at the upper right.

Vichy/Festival du Théâtre Amateur, 1957

Lefor-Openo (Marie-Claire Lefort, 1931–1971, and Marie-Francine Oppeneau, 1931–2023)
Poster House Permanent Collection

- The French Federation of Amateur Theater Societies (today, Companies) is a national network of nonprofessional acting troupes dating back to the early 20th century. This poster advertises its 50th-anniversary festival in Vichy.
- Many of Lefor-Openo's early posters are for events in the city of Vichy, Marie-Claire Lefort's hometown. While the two women certainly had talent, such commissions reflect the importance of Lefort's father's professional connections in securing early opportunities for them, work that probably would not have been available to other women poster designers at the time.
- This poster and others they created for Vichy also incorporate many of the motifs that would come to define their signature style within a few years, including the round-faced, sassy female figure and the jaunty, gestural line drawings.

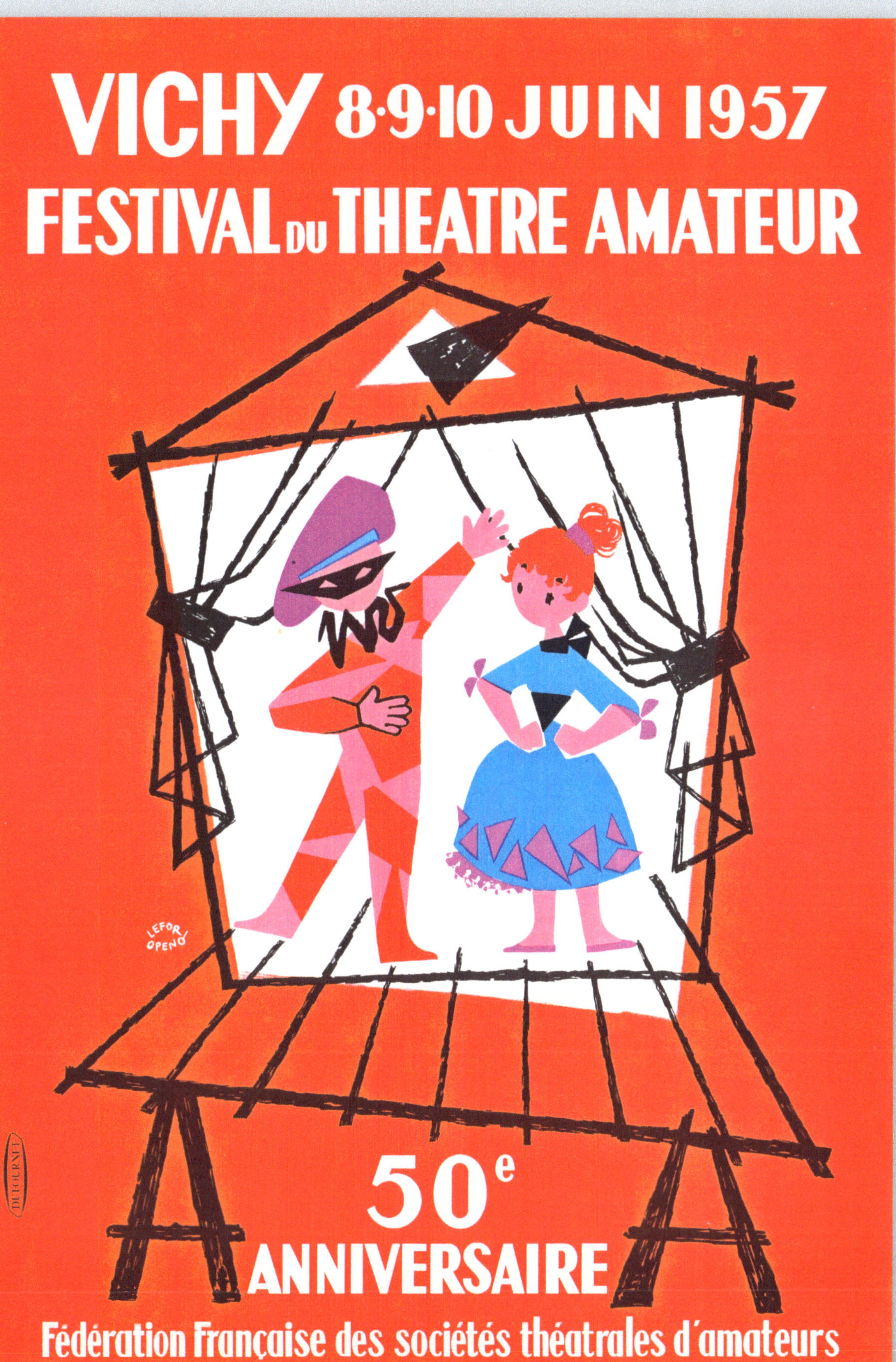
VICHY 8·9·10 JUIN 1957
FESTIVAL du THEATRE AMATEUR
LEFOR OPENO
50e
ANNIVERSAIRE
Fédération Française des sociétés théatrales d'amateurs

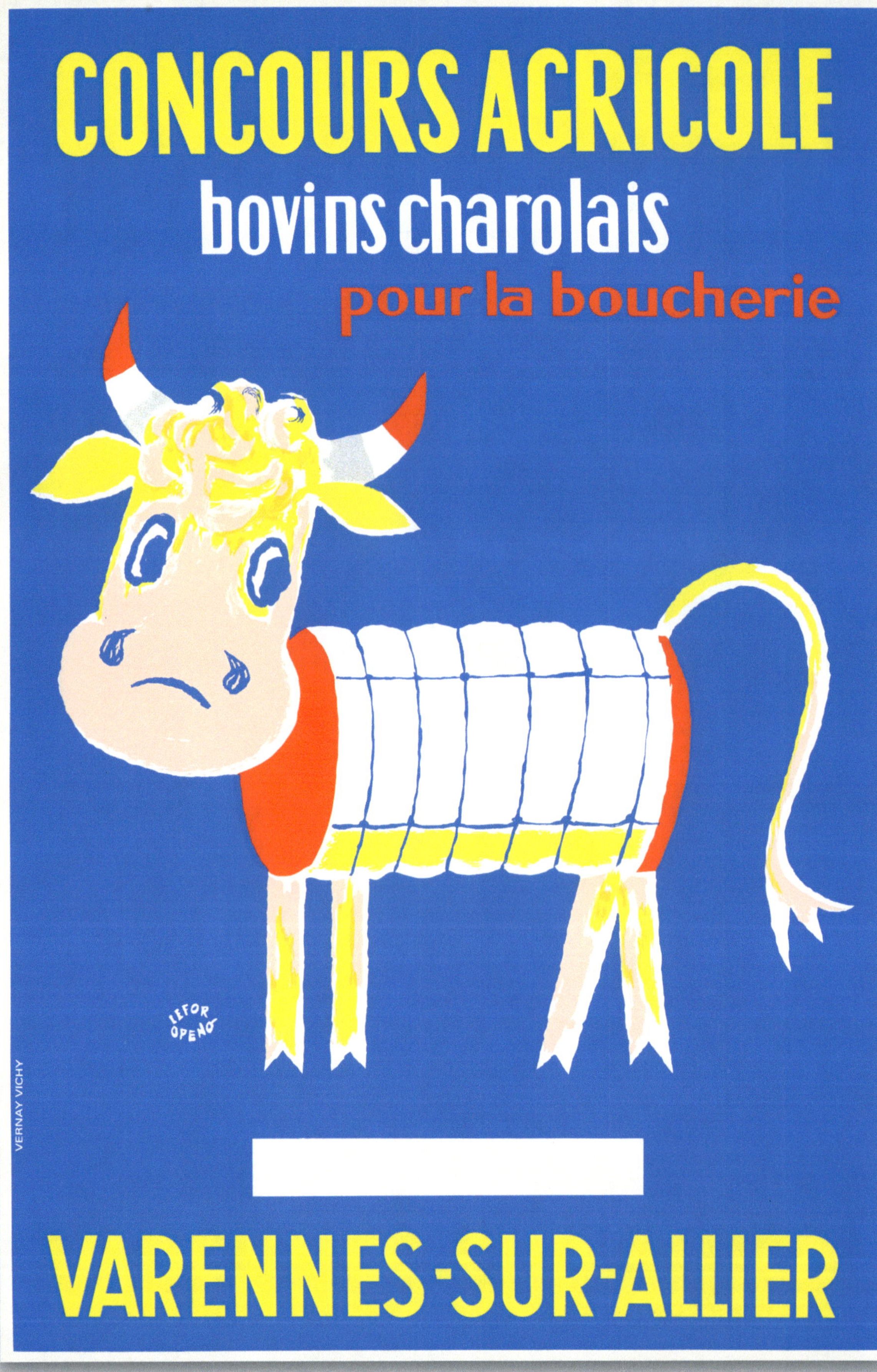
CONCOURS AGRICOLE
bovins charolais
pour la boucherie
LEFOR OPENO
VERNAY VICHY
VARENNES-SUR-ALLIER

Concours Agricole, c. 1958

Lefor-Openo (Marie-Claire Lefort, 1931–1971, and Marie-Francine Oppeneau, 1931–2023)

Poster House Permanent Collection

- World War II devastated much of the French agricultural system. Some sources claim that during the 1944 invasion of Normandy alone, more than 100,000 cattle died as collateral damage, in addition to the millions that perished during the course of the war. This destruction made France, once a large exporter of meat and dairy products, reliant on foreign food sources, a reality that the government actively attempted to fix by allocating generous resources toward the rebuilding of the industry.
- Agricultural fairs like the one advertised in this poster were an opportunity to draw the public's attention to France's various farming sectors, not only providing a platform for financially supporting them but also encouraging a sense of national pride around them.
- Varennes-sur-Allier is located in the Vichy region, indicating that Lefor-Openo may have been given this commission due to Lefort's family connection to the area. The design was deemed impactful enough that it was reprinted to advertise a similar event in 1991.
- Here, Lefor-Openo presents a darkly humorous image of an unhappily startled cow, its body trussed for roasting. It is accompanied by the announcement that Charolais cattle will be the highlight of the event, all ready for slaughter. Charolais are France's most common type of beef breed, known for their pale color and pink noses.
- French poster designs of this period frequently incorporated anthropomorphic animals (an animal that takes on human characteristics), bright colors, and cheeky or funny scenarios. When creating this composition, Lefor-Openo would have been familiar with Raymond Savignac's iconic poster from the previous decade for Monsavon soap, also featuring a cow on a blue background. This image was reprinted several times and was so loved that when Savignac died in 2002, the company printed a farewell billboard in his honor featuring the design.

Concours International de la CISPM, 1959

Lefor-Openo (Marie-Claire Lefort, 1931–1971, and Marie-Francine Oppeneau, 1931–2023)

Collection of Fionn Halleman, France

- After World War II, the French population was eager to dissociate itself from its official wartime government that had openly collaborated with Nazi Germany. The spa town of Vichy in particular was in dire need of a rebrand in both domestic and international consciousness, as it had been the seat and namesake of the Vichy regime.
- In 1950, Pierre Coulon became the mayor of Vichy and immediately began an active campaign to recontextualize and modernize the city. He encouraged new developments around sports and culture, including the competition of the International Confederation of Popular Music Societies (today, the International Confederation of Music Societies) advertised in this poster.
- Like much of Lefor-Openo's work from this period, this poster presents nothing but optimism. It is even so bold as to lead with Germany's flag on the heraldic banner held by the trumpeter—a confident gesture, implying that the issues of the past are no longer a concern for Vichy.

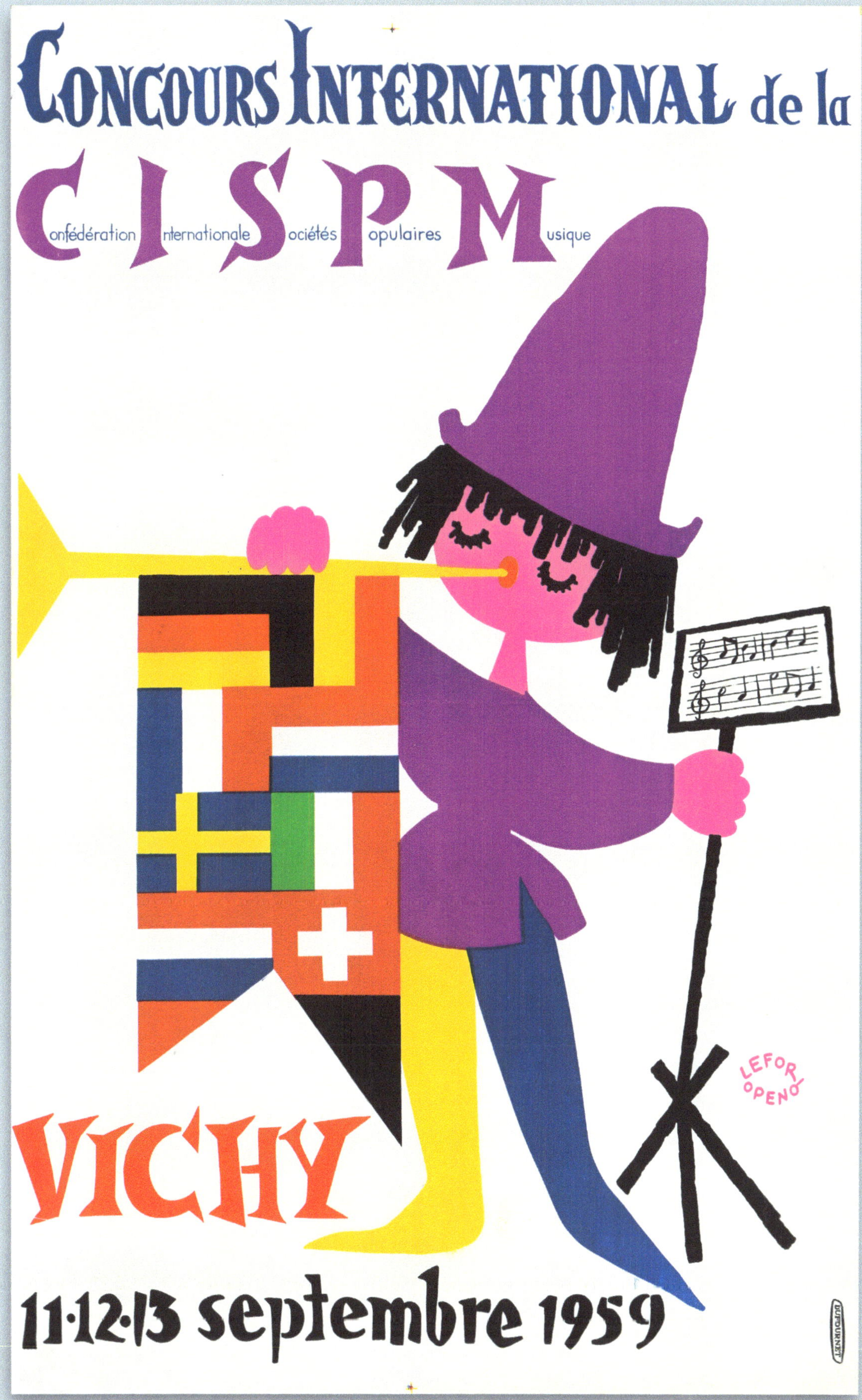

Concours International de la
CISPM
Confédération Internationale Sociétés Populaires Musique
LEFOR OPENO
VICHY
11·12·13 septembre 1959

GUY DE LA VASSELAIS
THE MAN BEHIND THE WONDERLAND STYLE

Michael Lellouche

"Paris! Paris outraged! Paris broken! Paris martyred! But Paris liberated!"

General Charles de Gaulle's words at the Liberation of Paris on August 25, 1944, sounded like the turning of a page, the opening of a horizon of relief. As World War II entered its final year, France was exhausted and devastated. Between 1948 and 1951, the American government poured billions of dollars in financial aid into the reconstruction of European nations through the Marshall Plan. This support enabled the steel, automobile, agricultural machinery, and energy industries to relaunch their activities. France (like its German and Italian neighbors) entered the era known as *Les Trente Glorieuses* (The Glorious Thirty)—three decades of exceptional economic growth. The French population, lagging the Americans by several decades in this respect, now fully embraced consumer culture. Jazz, chewing gum, and American films erased the dark years. Joy and optimism were everywhere. Farewell hardship! The whole family could now travel by car, and machines relieved Madame of domestic labor (gender roles remained largely traditional). Farewell gloom! Farewell deprivation! All you had to do was turn on the television to watch game shows as you ate chocolate and cookies while sipping on soda. These new delights were all accompanied and amplified by advertising.

With their colorful illustrations and smiling, doll-like characters, the posters of the female design team Lefor-Openo perfectly embodied this new lifestyle. But they were far from the only poster artists to adopt this kind of cheerful, regressive approach; in fact, their compositions reflected a broader advertising trend that had swept like a tidal wave across the walls of French cities since the early 1950s. The sleek Art Deco lines, powerful modernist geometries, and elegance that had characterized the styles of prewar masters like A.M. Cassandre were no longer in fashion. Childish motifs now symbolized primal joy and collective optimism, sweeping away dull reality. Consumerism turned passersby into overgrown children; new household appliances and cars were promoted almost as if they were toys for adults. Advertising posters embraced fun and cute imagery: They were humorous, light, like cartoons or fairy tales populated by elves and sprites, conjuring realms in which everyday worries had no place. It was a parallel world, a waking dream, like Alice's Wonderland (Disney's animated version of Lewis Carroll's classic children's book was released in France in 1951). This "Wonderland" style, one that combined fantasy and absurdity, was largely the work of a man who remained in the shadows, playing the role of producer and conductor, rallying a wide range of talented illustrators around his vision: the printer and publisher Guy de La Vasselais.

If his name sounds familiar, it is perhaps because La Vasselais was associated with Raymond Savignac, the illustrator who most famously embodied the Wonderland spirit, eclipsing others in the collective memory—the tree that hid the forest. Savignac created dozens of posters for the Établissements de La Vasselais advertising company. However, Guy de La Vasselais himself was a larger-than-life character with an extraordinary history. Born in 1902, he fought in World War I at the age of just 15 as one of the 1,000 youngest soldiers and returned from the battlefield with the Croix de Guerre. After earning a law degree, he ran an agricultural farm before launching his advertising business in 1934. The venture quickly became successful, not least due to the work of designers Pierre and Jacques Bellenger, who created the legendary posters for the Quinquina Bourin aperitif in 1936. During World War II, La Vasselais, temporarily shuttering his advertising company, was involved in the Resistance and, as an officer in the French army, became the head of tactical liaison to General Patton's Third Army. He again received the Croix de Guerre and the highest French and Allied military decorations. In 1945, he began a political career as the mayor of Saint-Symphorien-le-Château in the Loire region (a position he would hold for three decades), and in 1946 he created the Voix de la Liberté, a commemorative route of 710 miles marking the movement of Patton's troops from Normandy in France to Bastogne in Belgium. From 1946 onward, he headed an agricultural union and an agrochemical company, and in 1950 he relaunched the Établissements de La Vasselais.

By 1949, four years after the end of the war, the French economy was beginning to recover. An advertising Wonderland soon emerged, although its precise date of birth is difficult to establish because the new graphic style was never formally identified. Two small sparks, occurring a few months apart, however, mark a tentative point of departure. In 1945, Raymond Savignac—who had worked with Cassandre before the war—was hired by Robert Guérin, an advertising executive at the Consortium Général de Publicité (CGP), to produce leaflets for the cosmetics company L'Oréal (although his distinctive style did not really emerge in this context). In 1947, Guérin commissioned Savignac to design a small, playful poster with a low print run for Dalle, a beer from northern France owned by the family of the director of CGP. It features the colorful, stylized figure of a man shown upside down with the tagline "Elle vous remettra d'aplomb" (It will get you back on your feet). Meanwhile, Hervé Morvan, an illustrator 10 years Savignac's junior, had already designed about 15 film posters since the war. In 1948, he produced a cartoon-style magazine advertisement for Scandale corsetry: a man wearing an advertising sandwich board looks down and realizes that the image on it shows a woman in lingerie, and that her body appears to be superimposed on his own. This vibrant and humorous composition represented a true visual gag, introducing a new style to advertising.

A few months later, in 1949, a full-blown Wonderland would explode onto the walls of French cities, asserting its dual parentage. On one side was Morvan, with a poster for Gerline detergent (for the Noirclerc agency) in which the female figure recalls those in Derouet and Lesacq's 1939 posters for the National Lottery. Here, the detergent foam becomes the silhouette of a smiling washerwoman; this transformation of product into body (already present in the Scandale ad) became a recurring motif in this new realm of advertising. On the other side was Savignac. In June 1949, he exhibited poster maquettes with his friend Bernard Villemot at the Maison des Beaux-Arts in Paris. A laudatory article by Robert Guérin, published a year earlier in the French design journal *Publimondial*, had already aroused curiosity about this artist who was then struggling to secure commissions: "I weigh my words when I say that Savignac is the precursor, the man of tomorrow, the most popular poster artist of the century, currently living through his hour of unpopularity." Eugène Schueller, the founder of L'Oréal, visited the exhibition and discovered a maquette that had been rejected by the Monsavon soap brand, which he owned. He immediately decided to use it. The Monsavon poster—with no slogan—features a cow whose udders are transformed into a soap bar, a funny idea emphasizing its milk content; the image subverts standard cosmetics advertising featuring pretty women doing their makeup and, once again, merges body and product. The poster was pasted, to much acclaim, all over the streets of Paris. At the age of 41, Savignac achieved instant fame and chose to exploit it as a freelancer.

In early 1950, Morvan created a poster for Kwatta chocolate (again for the Noirclerc agency) showing a child licking fingers made of chocolate bars—body and product fused yet again. This image faintly evokes the Surrealist art of René Magritte, who was Belgian—like the Kwatta brand. Savignac responded with a poster for Astral paint, showing two men, one standing on his head, as they paint each other from head to toe. In just four posters, the Wonderland style had been launched with this dual paternity. Guy de La Vasselais, with his keen eye for talent, relaunched his advertising company that year by signing Hervé Morvan to an exclusive and lucrative contract. The Établissements de La Vasselais inaugurated, with a Perrier campaign for which Morvan created four gigantic posters, the style that would become its trademark. Savignac, meanwhile, drew a surreal image of a woman knitting herself from wool for the Belgian company Laines d'Aoust, pushing the body-product fusion idea to its extreme. From 1951 onward, Morvan produced posters for a succession of campaigns, including Grey Poupon and Maille mustards as well as Paillette Pils beer, progressively softening his line and moving closer to Savignac's style. In 1951, Savignac created a sheep unraveling into a ball of wool for the promotional Quinzaine de la laine (Wool Fortnight) and into a human mattress for Dunlopillo. In August 1951, fewer than two years after he designed the cow for Monsavon soap, Savignac received the Grand Prix de l'Affiche Française. In November, *Fortune* magazine devoted four pages to him, written by its art director, Leo Lionni, and his international reputation was sealed. There was further positive critical response from many countries, and Savignac became the uncontested poster king.

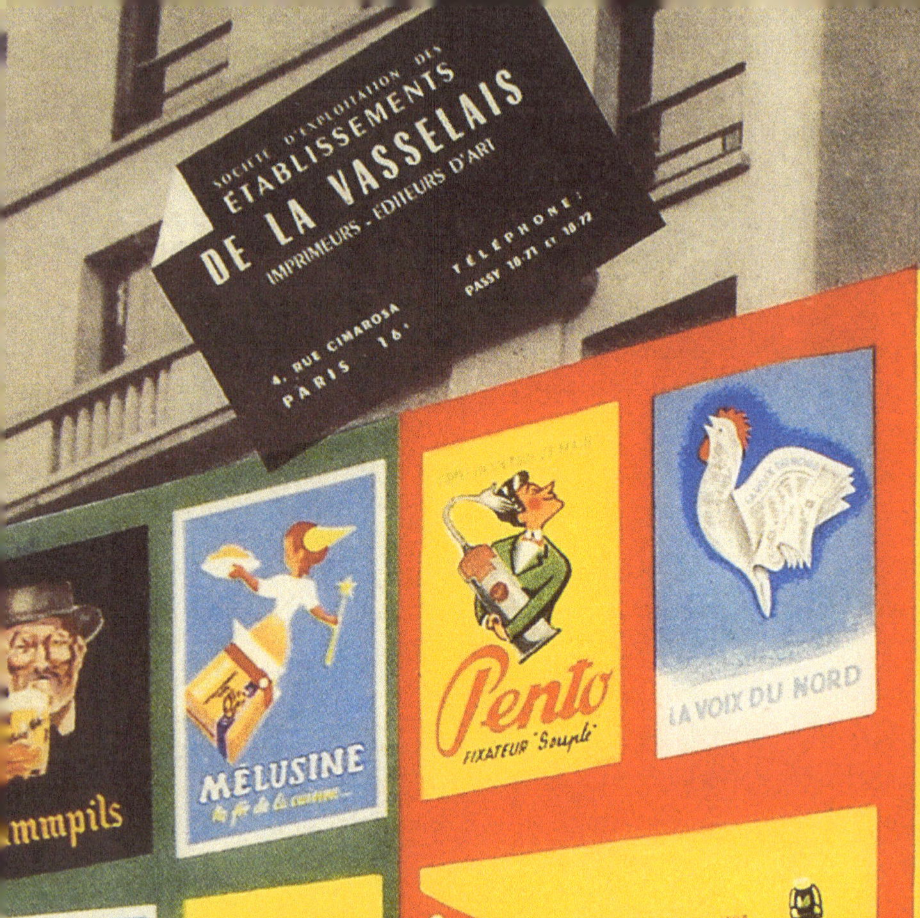

SOCIÉTÉ D'EXPLOITATION DES
ÉTABLISSEMENTS
DE LA VASSELAIS
IMPRIMEURS - ÉDITEURS D'ART
4, RUE CIMAROSA
PARIS 16e
TÉLÉPHONE:
PASSY 18-71 ET 18-72
mmpils
MÉLUSINE
la fée de la cuisine...
Pento
FIXATEUR "Souple"
LA VOIX DU NORD

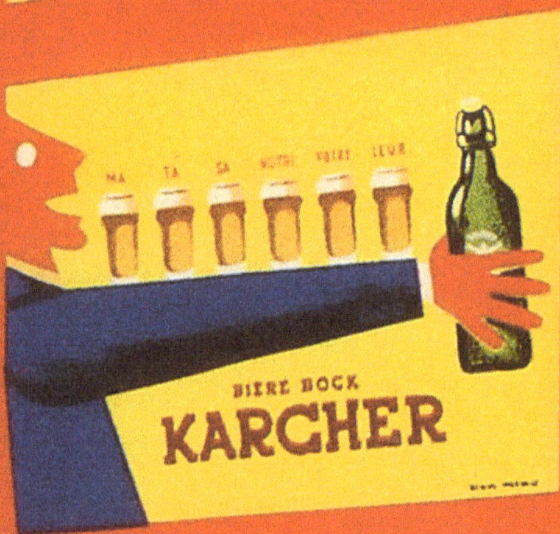

MA
TA
SA
NOTRE
VOTRE
LEUR
BIERE BOCK
KARCHER

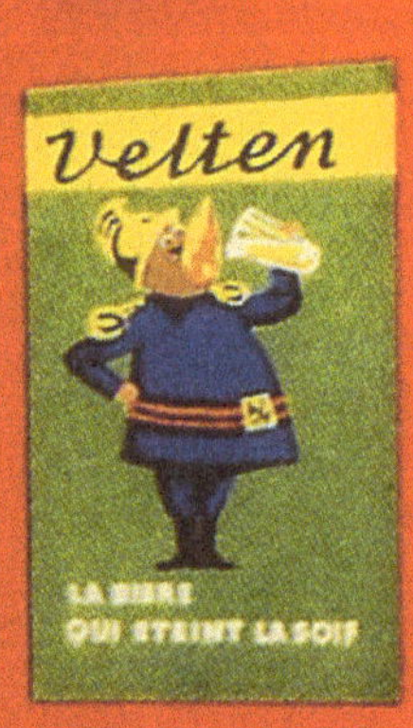

Velten
LA BIERE
QUI ETEINT LA SOIF

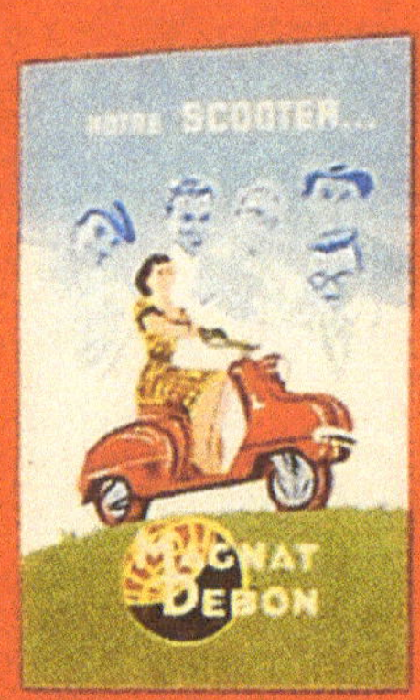

NOTRE SCOOTER...
DEBON

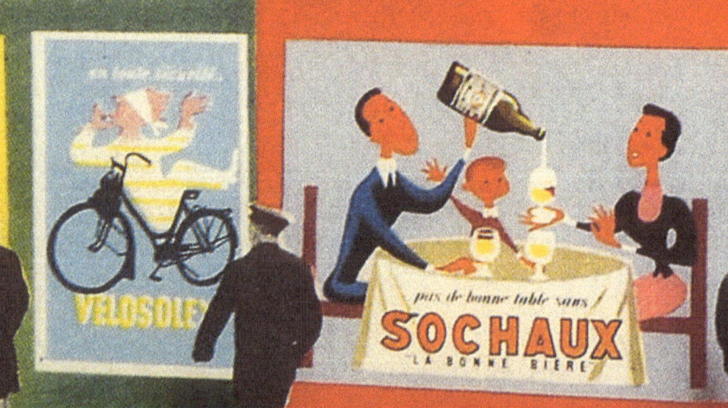

VELOSOLE
pas de bonne table sans
SOCHAUX
LA BONNE BIÈRE

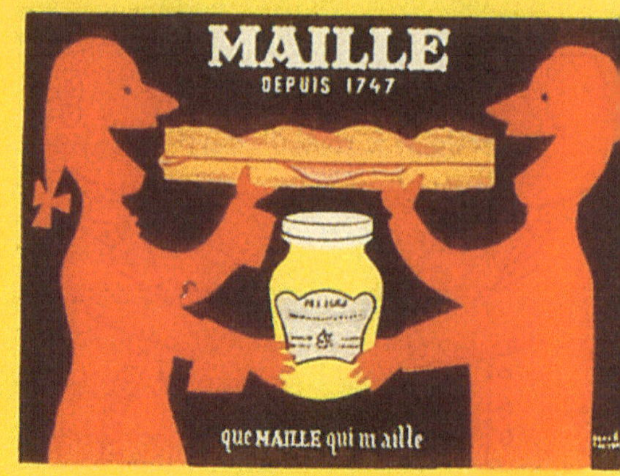

MAILLE
DEPUIS 1747
que MAILLE qui m'aille

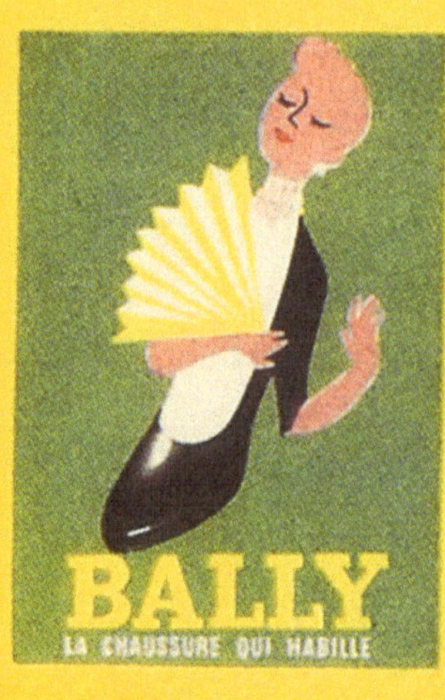

BALLY
LA CHAUSSURE QUI HABILLE

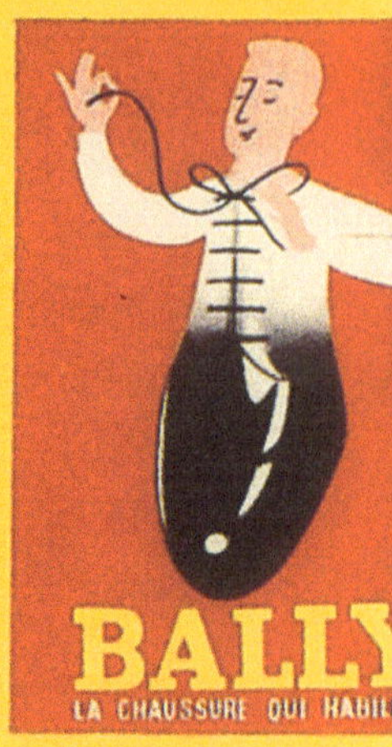

BALLY
LA CHAUSSURE QUI HABILL

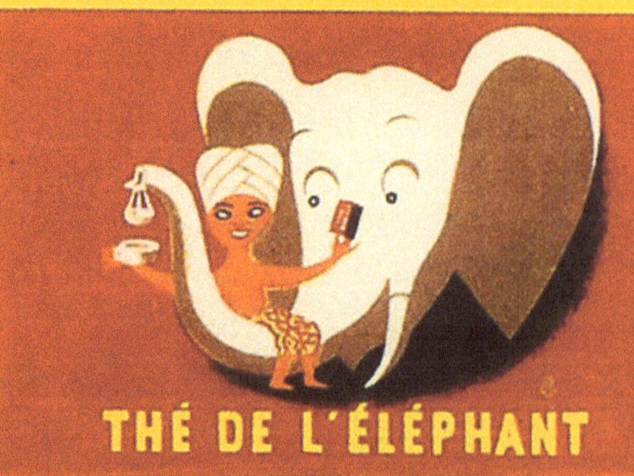

THÉ DE L'ÉLÉPHANT

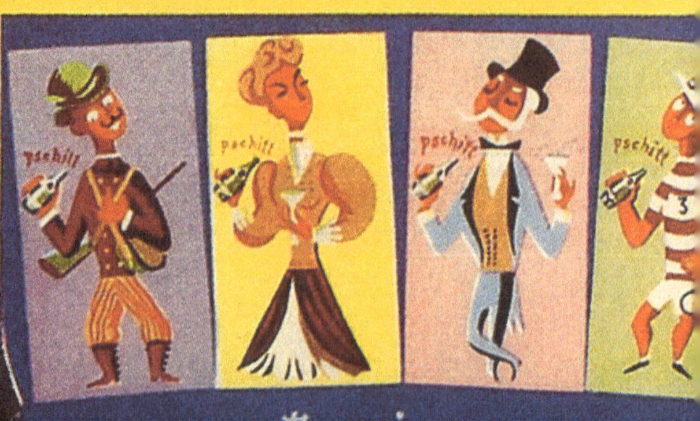

pschitt
pschitt
pschitt
pschitt
Perrier...

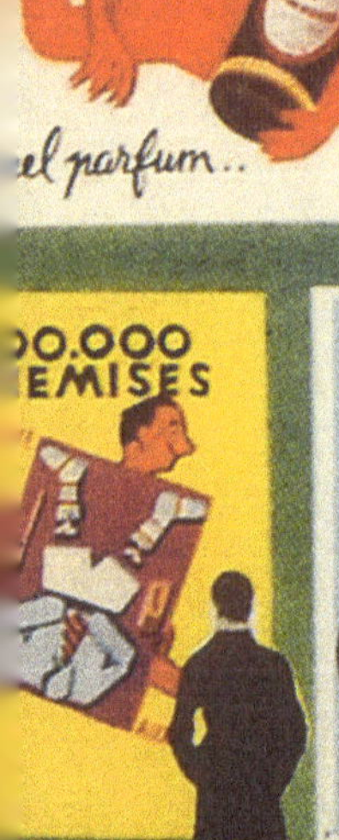

00.000
EMISES

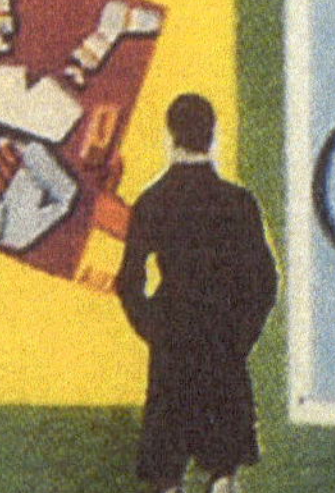

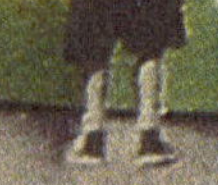

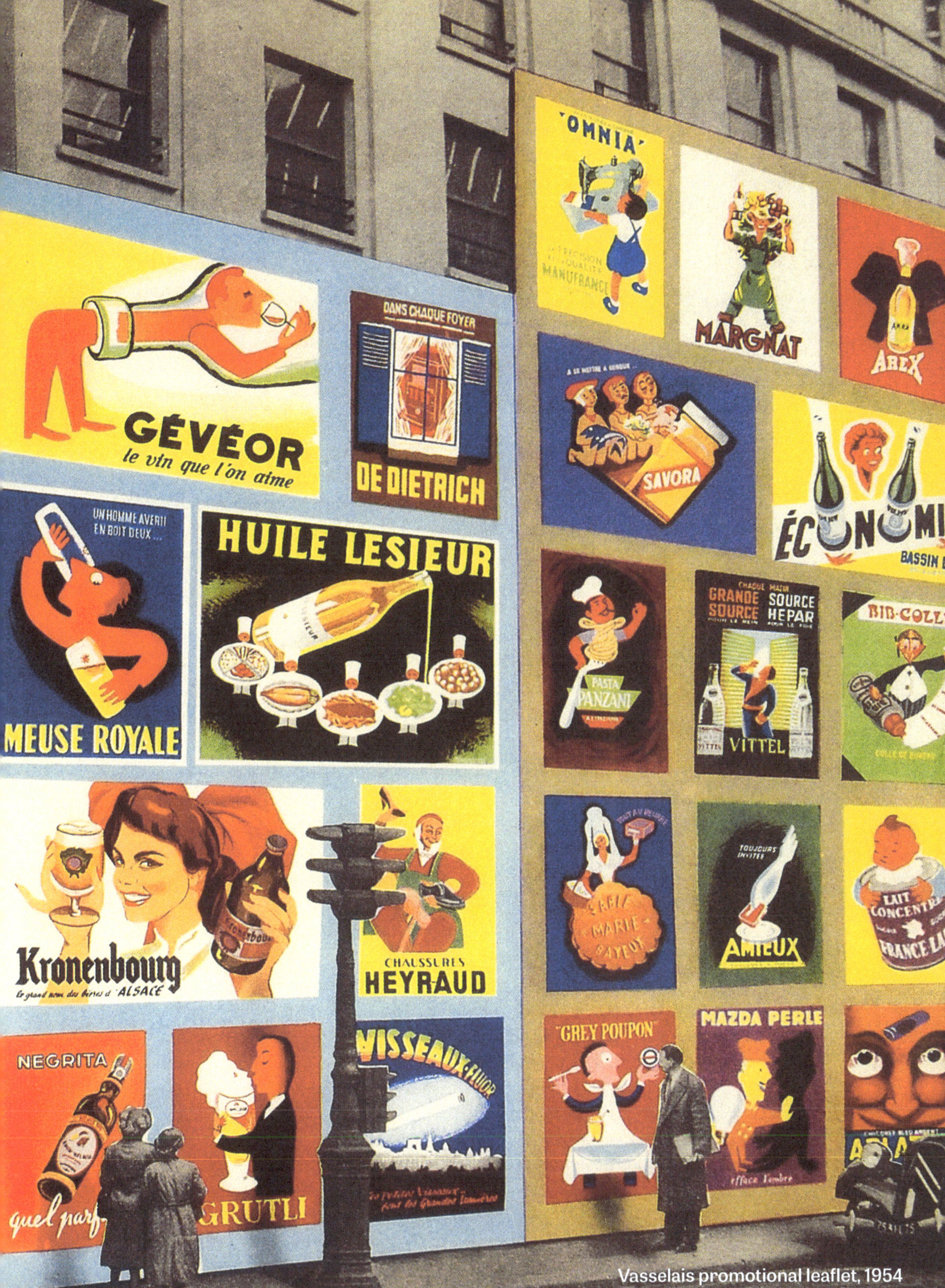

Vasselais promotional leaflet, 1954

Jeannot l'intrépide (Johnny the Giant Killer), the first major French animated feature film, was released at the end of 1950, and Albert Champeaux's graphic style and dreamlike universe established the Wonderland spirit on screen. The following year, Champeaux created Petit Mineur (Little Miner), a clone of Johnny dressed as a cheerful miner: the figure became the animated logo of the Jean Mineur advertising company and appeared in cinemas across France for decades. A few months later, Disney's *Alice in Wonderland* was released. All of this reinforced the aesthetic line defended by Guy de La Vasselais, whose company was rapidly expanding. Morvan worked on about 10 more campaigns in 1952, including those for Bally (characters merging with shoes) and Panzani pasta (a body shaped like a fork holding spaghetti). La Vasselais expanded his creative team, bringing back prewar designers who quickly adapted to the Wonderland style: the Bellenger brothers, Édouard Courchinoux, Robert Falcucci, and Charles Rohonyi, whose playful style was close to Morvan's. He also recruited new talent: Georges Nicolitch, Delbosco, and Jean Desaleux in 1953; and André Roland and Jacques Auriac the following year. The company flourished, working for Danone, Philips, Brandt, Vittel, Evian, Mazda, Lesieur, and dozens of other major brands. La Vasselais published brochures promoting its services and creative team with the slogan "Qui affichera vendra" (If you advertise, you will sell) and almost never deviated from the Wonderland style, only occasionally hiring classic illustrators like Emmanuel Gaillard and Raymond Brenot for his more conservative clients.

By 1954, the Établissements de La Vasselais had produced 60 poster campaigns, and nearly 3 times that number by 1957. Some of Morvan's posters for the agency have since become icons, among them those for Gévéor (1953), featuring a man drinking wine with the upper half of his body inside a giant bottle—a play on scale like that in *Alice in Wonderland*; or Brandt (1955), a tall, narrow poster showing a giraffe's head emerging from the body of a penguin inside a refrigerator. Jacques Auriac gradually became as important as Morvan within the agency, and new illustrators kept arriving: Alain Wienc, Roland Omnès, and Onell and Roger Varenne. By 1957, an undercurrent emerged within Wonderland: Francis Saint-Geniès's characters evolved into almond-eyed dolls, perfectly suited to encouraging young girls' interest in household appliances. This "woman-child" aesthetic— contemporaneous with Rune Naito's characters and the kawaii style emerging in Japan—was adopted by Alain Gauthier and the Lefor-Openo team, who joined the new generation of designers.

Wonderland spread further, and competing agencies took it on as well. Since La Vasselais was not in a position to monopolize the market, new poster artists—among them René Ravo, Georges Amalric and Maurice Gouju, and Pierre-Paul Darigo—emerged at rival printer-publishers such as Bedos, Synergie, Gaillard, and Hénon. Even prewar illustrators whose original styles had been very different tried their hands at Wonderland: Jean Colin, Jean Carlu, Pierre Fix-Masseau, Pierre Lacroix (the creator of the *Bibi Fricotin* comic books), and even the great Paul Colin (Bosch refrigerators, Tac detergent) all imitated Savignac and Morvan in their own ways. By the mid-1960s,

La Vasselais had become unavoidable. The agency had produced nearly 1,000 campaigns in 15 years, and its artists were loyal. But one jewel was missing from its crown: Savignac himself. Finally, on February 1, 1964, Raymond Savignac signed an exclusive contract with the Établissements de La Vasselais. The terms were exceptional: a guaranteed monthly salary equivalent to 30 times a worker's minimum wage and 10 percent of the agency's revenues from his posters. He was also allowed to keep his established clients like Bic and Renault. This arrangement worked perfectly, and Savignac went on to produce around 60 posters over the next 10 years. La Vasselais had succeeded: his company was now home to a true all-star team of poster artists (even Bernard Villemot would join a few years later).

The 1973 oil crisis marked the end of the carefree era of *Les Trente Glorieuses*. Advertising suffered. The joyful Wonderland characters, disconnected from the new reality and perhaps worn out after 25 years of supremacy, lost their relevance. Advertising became increasingly dominated by photography rather than illustration. At La Vasselais, leadership passed to Guy's son Claude, who nonetheless remained faithful to illustration and to the remaining loyal artists. But annual commissions could now be counted on one hand, and the company attempted a few ventures into television advertising. In 1976, after the agency had produced more than 1,500 posters, Guy de La Vasselais finally crossed to the other side of the looking glass and his company disappeared. The artists who had worked for him were left not only orphaned but also unemployed. Many retired, while the younger ones retrained in press illustration or book-cover design. (Alain Gauthier became a major figure in children's literature, illustrating more than 30 books over 4 decades, several written by Michel Tournier). Guy de La Vasselais remains the man who made an entire generation dream, smile, and consume, helping them forget the wounds of war. For this achievement, he perhaps deserved yet another medal of honor.

THE NATIONAL LOTTERY

France's National Lottery was established in July 1933 as a creative means of funding the country's recovery from World War I, specifically to aid those who had been wounded in battle or whose farms had been destroyed. While most wounded war veterans were eligible for disability pensions, those with extreme facial injuries were exempt because their issues did not technically prevent them from performing physical labor. Known as the *gueules cassées* (the broken-jawed), this demographic banded together to assert that their disfigurements were accompanied by other serious health problems as well as social discrimination and that they therefore required official support.

While public lotteries had been prohibited in the country since 1836, the government realized that gambling was challenging to regulate and, more importantly, could be used to financially supplement weakened social systems in a struggling economy. The new lottery was intended to be a temporary solution; 60 percent of the profits from the sale of tickets went back to the general public as prize money, while 40 percent was distributed to those in need. Unexpectedly, the first lottery proved incredibly popular: Demand for tickets far exceeded the number produced, and subsequent draws were immediately scheduled. Within a few months, nearly half of the adult population of the country was participating, establishing the National Lottery as a useful addition to the postwar French welfare system.

The National Lottery continued to operate throughout World War II, funding a wartime relief organization. Its purpose changed slightly after the Liberation of France in 1944; beneficiaries now included displaced families, war veterans, and orphaned children. In the early 1950s, the prewar tradition of commissioning a poster for each special draw also resumed. In 1954, the *tiercé* (a type of horse-racing bet) was legalized, drawing attention (and participants) away from the lottery. To combat this competition, Charles Léonnet, the newly appointed secretary general of the National Lottery, sought out fresh talent to reinvigorate the program. Of the many potential new poster designs, he chose a work by Lefor-Openo to represent a new era. This decision launched a professional partnership that would gradually document many of the major social, economic, and political developments in France over the next 12 years.

Loterie Nationale, 1955
Lefor-Openo (Marie-Claire Lefort, 1931–1971, and Marie-Francine Oppeneau, 1931–2023)
Poster House Permanent Collection

Loterie Nationale, 1955
Lefor-Openo (Marie-Claire Lefort, 1931–1971, and Marie-Francine Oppeneau, 1931–2023)
Poster House Permanent Collection

- While the National Lottery continued to run through most of World War II, its posters were printed on increasingly cheaper paper with dour colors and compositions that typically emphasized suffering or charitable need. After the Liberation in 1944, the tradition of advertising individual draws was paused; however, when it resumed in the early 1950s, the lottery needed a new, more optimistic image, and its organizers put out a call for artists to submit poster designs.
- While it is unclear how Lefor-Openo met Yves Galichon (whose name appears as their agent on the left edge of this composition), he represented much of their early work and is credited with introducing them to Charles Léonnet of the National Lottery. Léonnet was charmed by their designs and granted them two commissions in rapid succession.
- Printed respectively in the spring and summer of 1955, these two posters brought a new humor to the National Lottery, demonstrating what a pirate and a gangster would do on vacation with their prize money (one knits a scarf out of rope riggings while the other turns his shotgun into a flute).

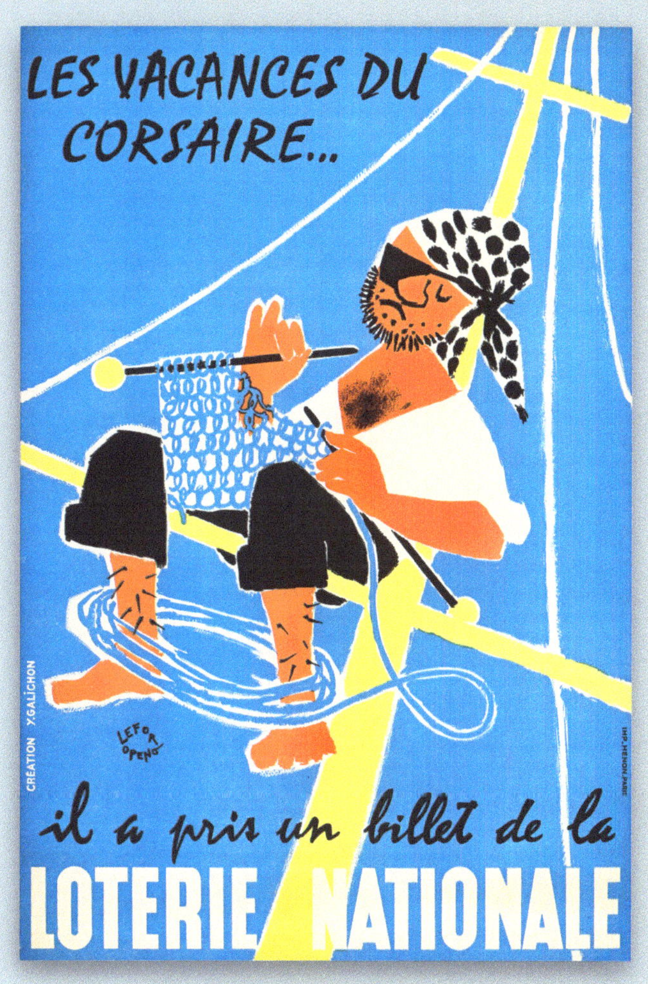
LES VACANCES DU
CORSAIRE...
il a pris un billet de la
LOTERIE NATIONALE
CRÉATION Y.GALICHON

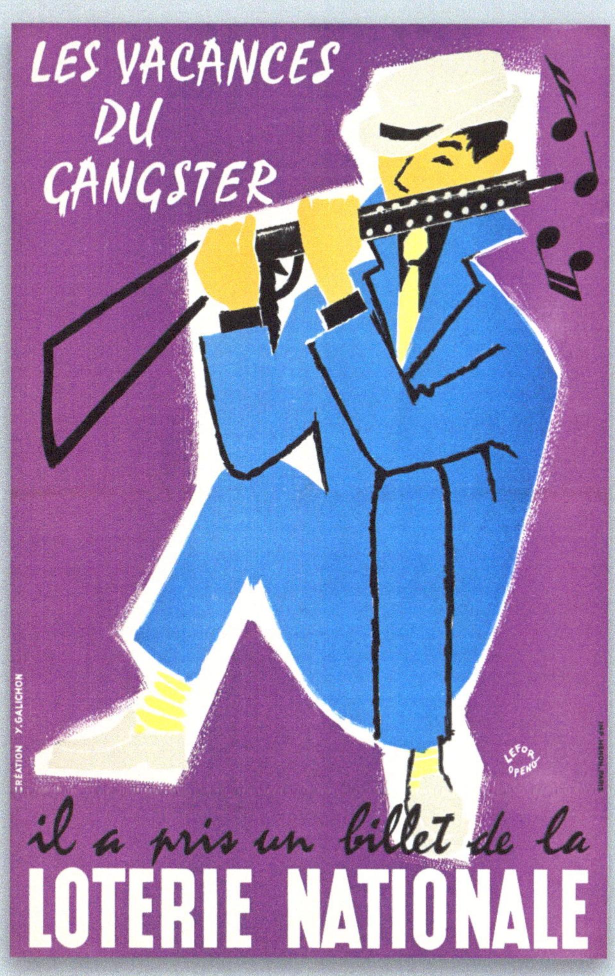
LES VACANCES
DU
GANGSTER
il a pris un billet de la
LOTERIE NATIONALE
CRÉATION Y.GALICHON

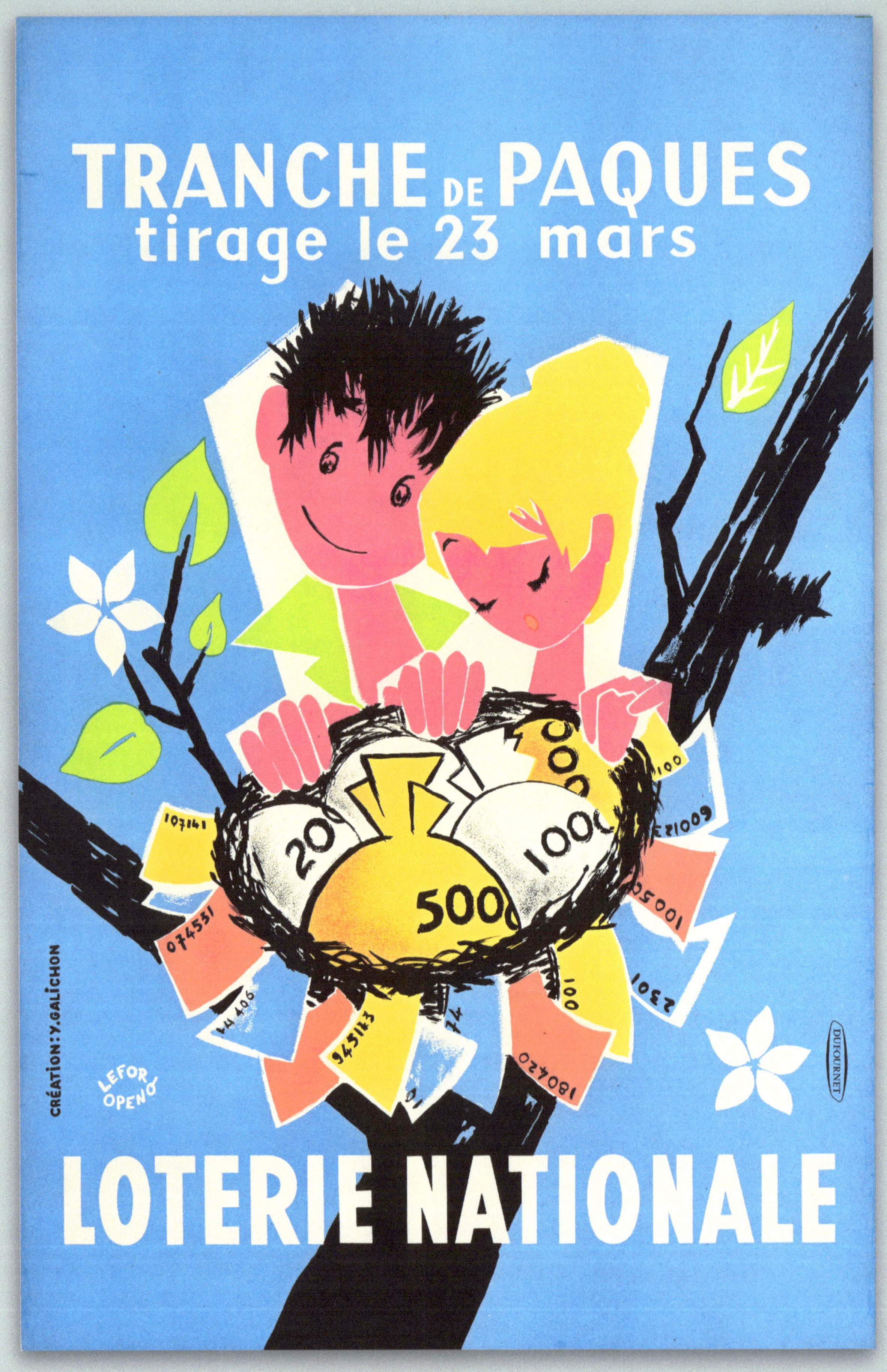
TRANCHE DE PAQUES
tirage le 23 mars
LOTERIE NATIONALE
CRÉATION: Y. GALICHON
LEFOR OPENO
DUFOURNET

Loterie Nationale, 1956

Lefor-Openo (Marie-Claire Lefort, 1931–1971, and Marie-Francine Oppeneau, 1931–2023)
Poster House Permanent Collection

- In addition to the weekly lottery draw that happened every Wednesday, special draws were issued for holidays and other notable events. This poster advertises the Easter lottery with an image of a young couple cooing over their nest of tickets filled with "eggs" of prize money.
- This design was eye-catching enough to warrant a mention in *Vente et Publicité*, a periodical focusing on the best in advertising design. It was described as especially "fresh" compared to other posters in circulation at the time. For a relatively unknown and new poster partnership, especially one composed of two women, this was unusually early and important praise, providing them with credibility among their mostly male peers.
- By 1956, Lefor-Openo's relationship with the National Lottery had been solidified. While the organization still required all designs to be submitted as part of a public "competition," the number of designers who worked regularly for it implies that this rule was mostly a formality. Lefor-Openo would continue to produce work for the lottery until 1960.

Loterie Nationale, 1956

Lefor-Openo (Marie-Claire Lefort, 1931–1971, and Marie-Francine Oppeneau, 1931–2023)

Poster House Permanent Collection

- Although it dates back to the 18th century, the story of Robinson Crusoe is a classic that would have been widely known by all French citizens in the 1950s. It was also the subject of a critically successful 1954 film adaptation by the avant-garde director Luis Buñel.
- Accompanied by the tagline "the luck of Robinson," the poster features an imagined scene based on plot points in the story. Crusoe, in ragged clothes, sits on his island with his pet parrot while the West African enslaved man he has named "Friday" triumphantly presents him with two bowls of prize money. In the original book, Friday and Crusoe form an unequal friendship in order to escape the island, that problem seemingly being solved here, since they have just won the lottery.
- This type of racialized imagery was common in France, and much of the French population still believed in the *mission civilisatrice* (civilizing mission) as a rationale for colonial practices. At the same time, this poster was produced during a period when France had recently relinquished parts of its empire, including Tunisia and Morocco, and was facing increasing tensions in its hold over Algeria and sub-Saharan Africa.

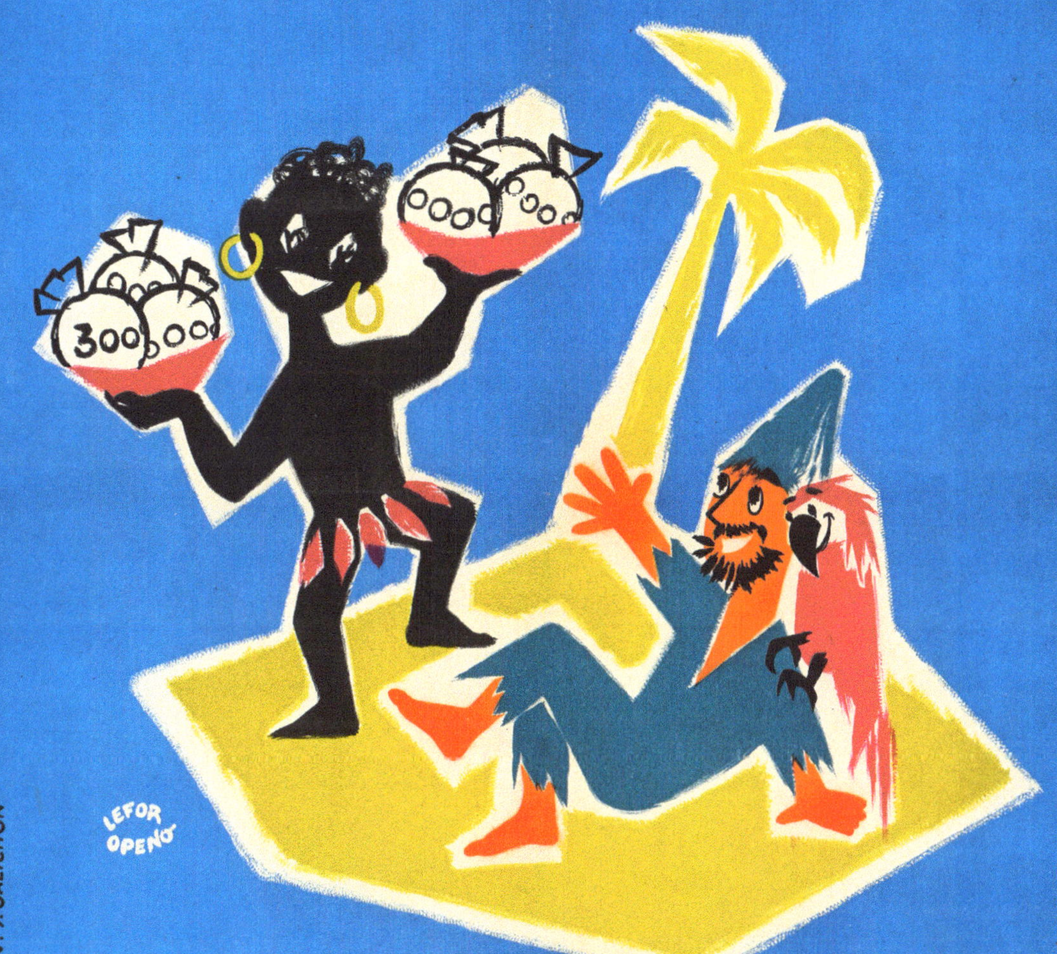
LOTERIE NATIONALE
Vendredi, chance de Robinson
300
LEFOR OPENO
CRÉATION : Y. GALICHON
IMP. HENON, 11, r. Stendhal, Paris
Vendredi 13
votre DOUBLE CHANCE
TIRAGE LE 18 AVRIL 1956

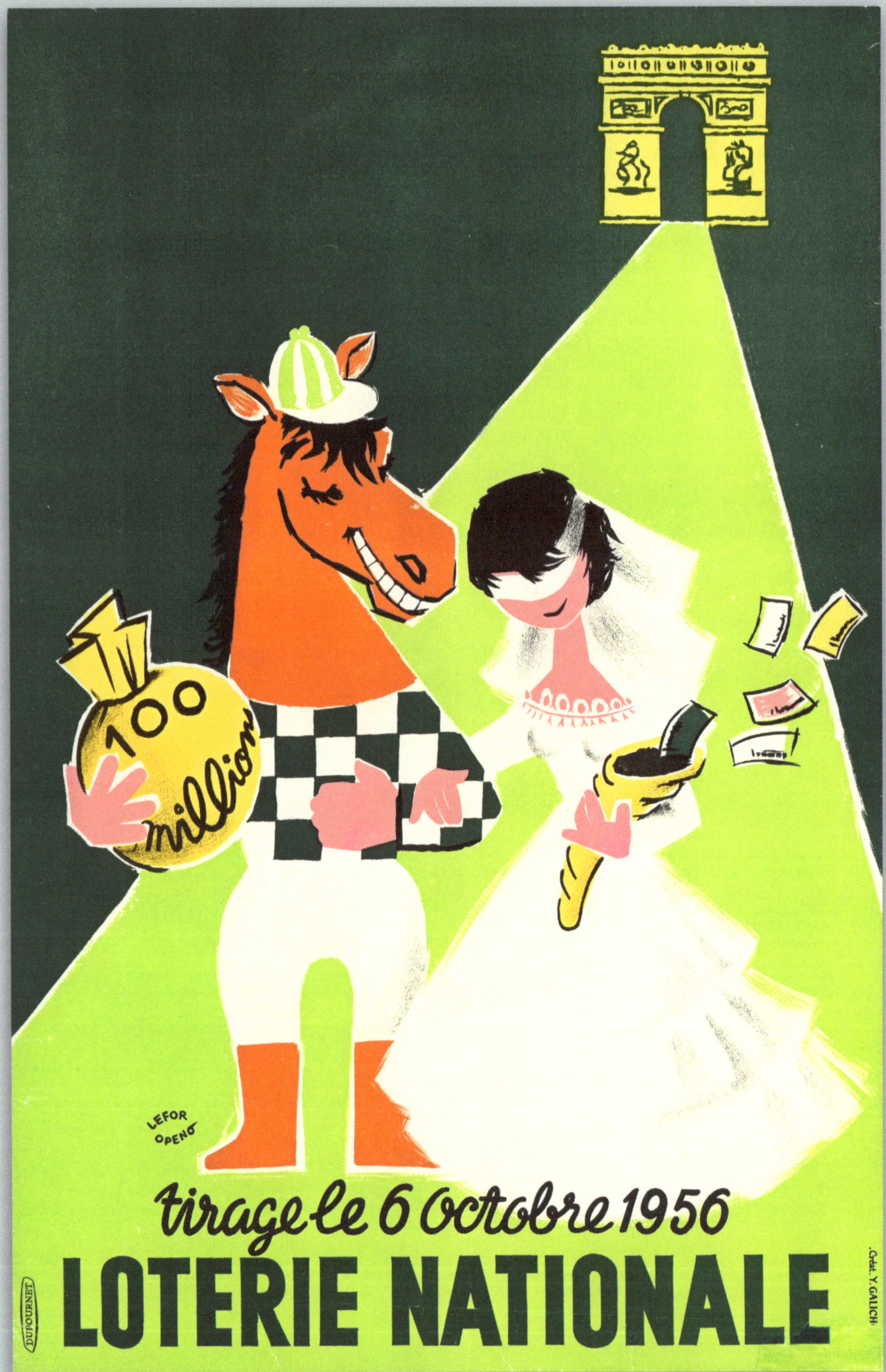
100
million
LEFOR
OPENO
tirage le 6 Octobre 1956
LOTERIE NATIONALE
DUFOURNET
Créat. Y. GALICH

Loterie Nationale, 1956

Lefor-Openo (Marie-Claire Lefort, 1931–1971, and Marie-Francine Oppeneau, 1931–2023)

Poster House Permanent Collection

- With the introduction in 1954 of the *tiercé* (a type of bet in horse racing in which participants try to predict the first three horses to cross the finish line), the National Lottery lost its monopoly on gambling. Even before then, though, it attempted to capitalize on the popularity of the sport by organizing specialized draws for some of the major Paris races, including the Prix de l'Arc de Triomphe alluded to in this poster.
- Here, a horse in jockey silks leads the blindfolded figure representing chance or fortune as his bride down an aisle of lush, green racing lawn along the Champes-Elysées, away from the Arc de Triomphe. She carries a cornucopia of tickets as her bouquet while he cradles a hefty bag of prize money.
- This type of surreal, anthropomorphic imagery was common in French poster designs of the time, offering a level of humor and escapism during an otherwise turbulent and uncertain political and social period.

Loterie Nationale, 1957

Lefor-Openo (Marie-Claire Lefort, 1931–1971, and Marie-Francine Oppeneau, 1931–2023)

Poster House Permanent Collection

- Printed for a special springtime drawing, this poster shows a woman in folk costume picking flowers made out of lottery tickets while carrying a basket full of prize money. Her features anticipate what would become Lefor-Openo's signature character for the rest of their career: a charming, round-faced lady with a beauty mark under her left eye. Her features were likely inspired by the work of Jean-Gabriel Domergue, whose popular paintings of pretty women with almond-shaped eyes were reproduced as prints in the hundreds of thousands and hung in many French homes throughout the 1950s.
- The phrase "Cueillez dès aujourd'hui" beneath the title of the poster is taken from famed Renaissance poet Pierre de Ronsard's *Sonnets pour Hélène* (1578), in which he encourages the reader to "gather today the roses of life." Here, the words urge the viewer to buy a lottery ticket without hesitation.
- Around the time this poster was printed, Marc Dufournet, the publisher of the National Lottery's many advertisements, replaced Yves Galichon as Lefor-Openo's agent, promoting their work to the secretary general of the organization as well as to other corporations. Less than a year after their first published design, the pair had acquired notable representation and were about to achieve national success.
- This poster in particular set the tone for the future of Lefor-Openo's career. The cheery optimism, bright colors, and smiling female figure aligned with the country's postwar self-image, one that exuded renewal and economic success. With the help of Dufournet's promotional efforts, this figure caught the attention of other companies that wanted to imbue their advertisements with similar lightheartedness.

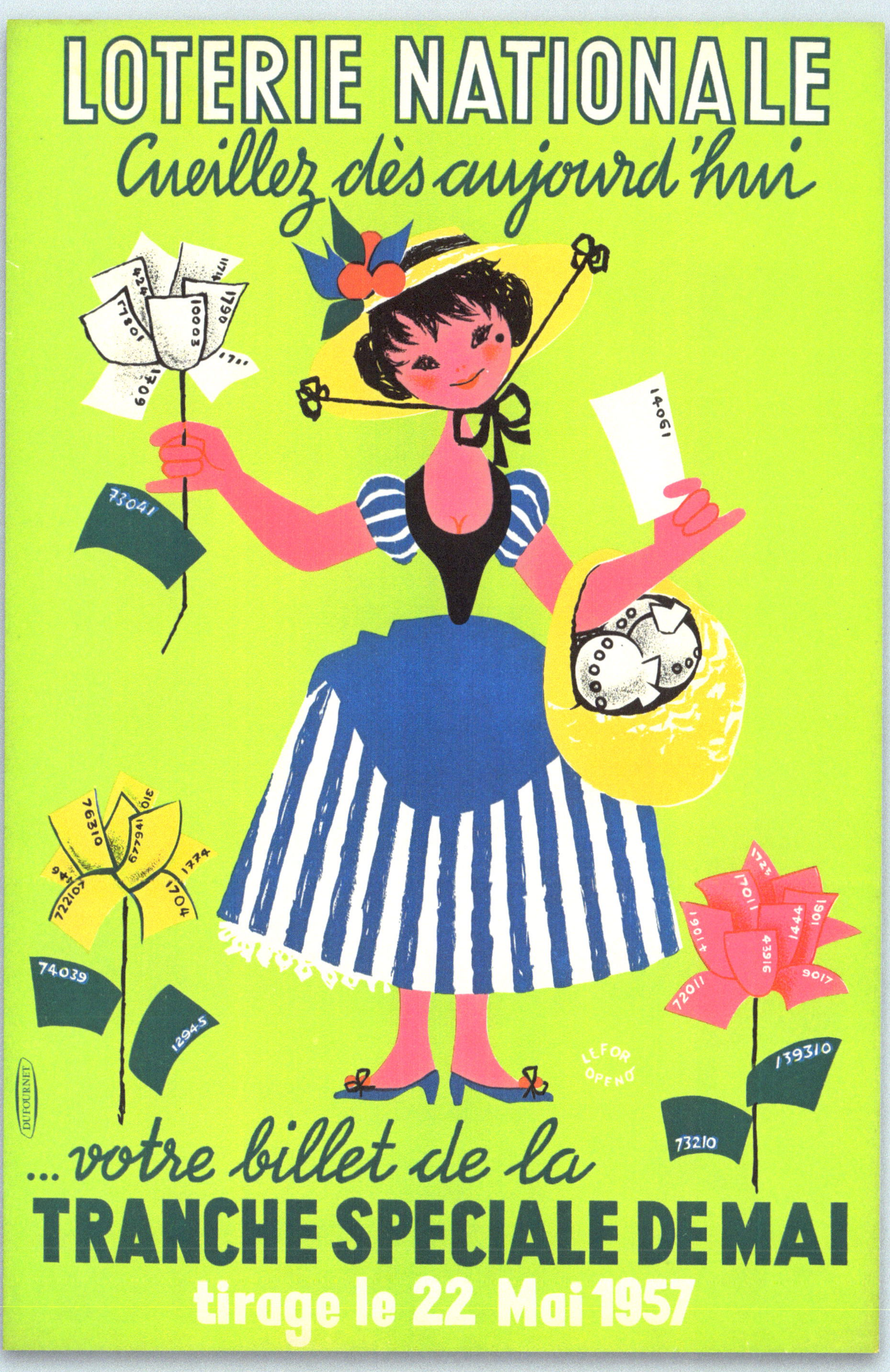
LOTERIE NATIONALE
Cueillez dès aujourd'hui
...votre billet de la
TRANCHE SPECIALE DE MAI
tirage le 22 Mai 1957
LEFOR OPENO
DUFOURNET

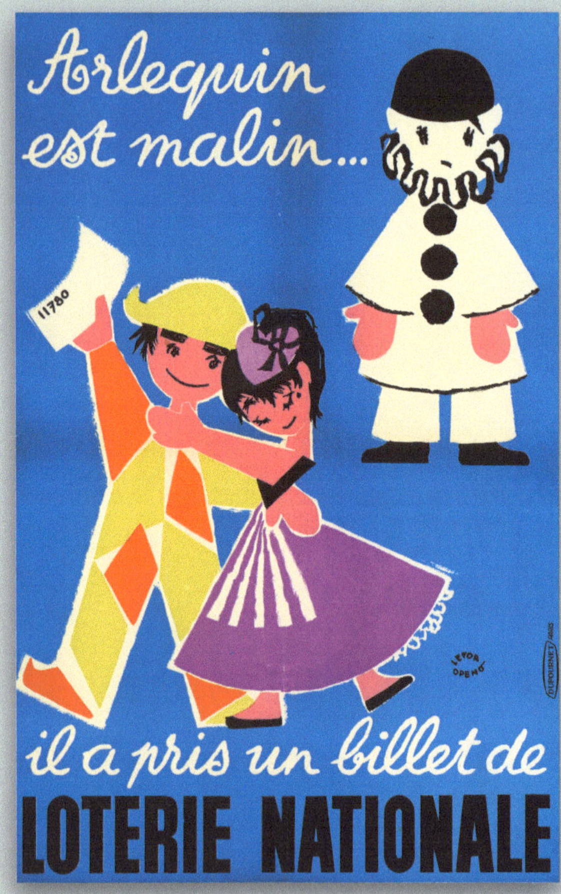

Arlequin
est malin...
11780
il a pris un billet de
LOTERIE NATIONALE

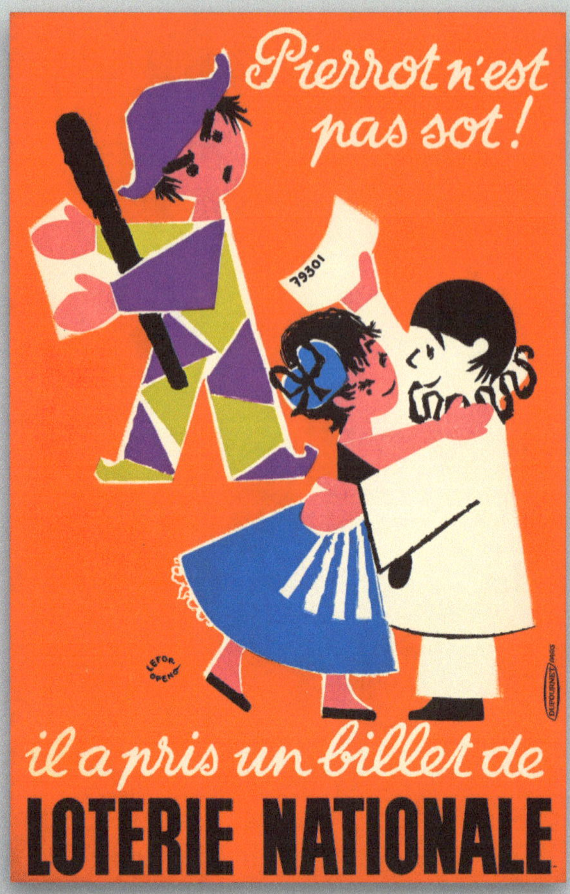

Pierrot n'est
pas sot !
79301
il a pris un billet de
LOTERIE NATIONALE

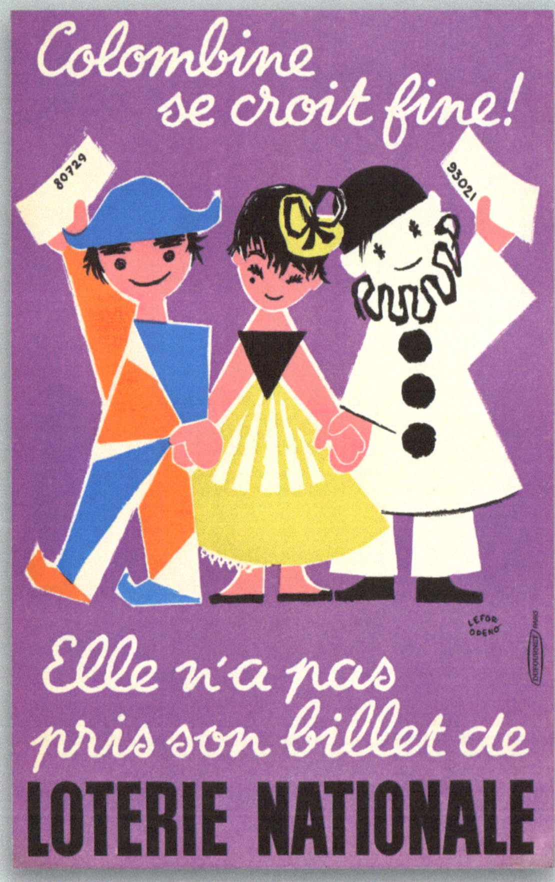

Colombine
se croit fine !
80729
93021
Elle n'a pas
pris son billet de
LOTERIE NATIONALE

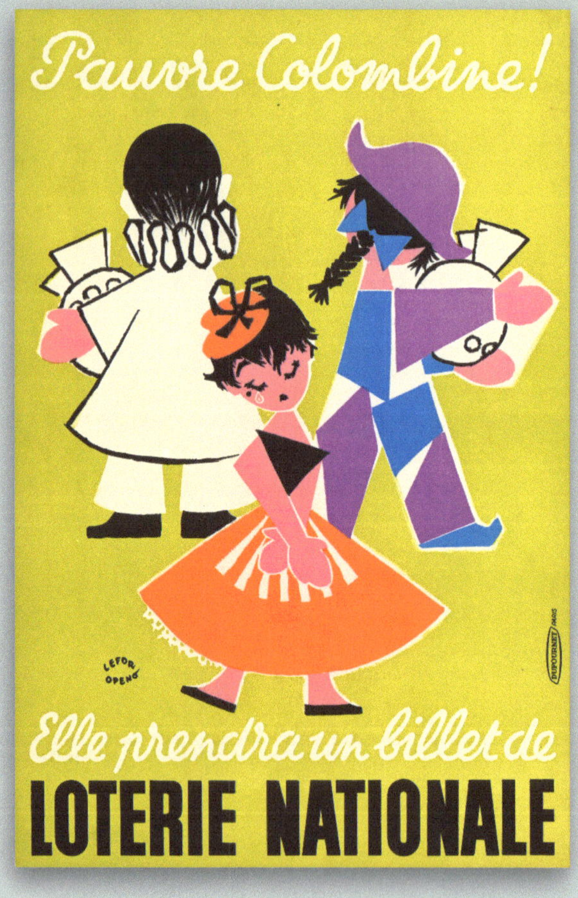

Pauvre Colombine !
Elle prendra un billet de
LOTERIE NATIONALE

Loterie Nationale, 1957
Lefor-Openo (Marie-Claire Lefort, 1931–1971, and Marie-Francine Oppeneau, 1931–2023)
Poster House Permanent Collection

Loterie Nationale, 1957
Lefor-Openo (Marie-Claire Lefort, 1931–1971, and Marie-Francine Oppeneau, 1931–2023)
Poster House Permanent Collection

Loterie Nationale, 1957
Lefor-Openo (Marie-Claire Lefort, 1931–1971, and Marie-Francine Oppeneau, 1931–2023)
Poster House Permanent Collection

Loterie Nationale, 1957
Lefor-Openo (Marie-Claire Lefort, 1931–1971, and Marie-Francine Oppeneau, 1931–2023)
Poster House Permanent Collection

- This series of four posters was printed in succession over a few weeks and uses the popular characters of commedia dell'arte to tell a story about why people should always buy their own lottery tickets.
- While it originated in 16th-century Italy, commedia dell'arte became a popular form of theater in France, drawing on a group of stock characters, most famously Harlequin, Colombina, and Pierrot. These three were often positioned in a love triangle that ended in tragedy, and they were frequently adopted by advertisers in posters to sell products as varied as bicycles and alcohol.
- Here, the posters show Colombina flirting with Harlequin and Pierrot respectively in the hope of sharing some of their prize money if they win the lottery. By the third image, she has successfully seduced both of them and "thinks she's clever"; however, the final design shows both men walking away from her, winnings in hand, as she weeps over the folly of not buying her own ticket.
- A popular French expression states that a person can be lucky in love or gambling, but not both. It would have been understood that while Colombina mourns the loss of both men in the final poster, she will soon have a winning lottery ticket.

Loterie Nationale, 1957

Lefor-Openo (Marie-Claire Lefort, 1931–1971, and Marie-Francine Oppeneau, 1931–2023)

Poster House Permanent Collection

- Printed for the annual August vacation draw, this poster shows a young couple in matching Breton sweaters brandishing winning lottery tickets as they soar above France in hot-air balloons shaped like purses of prize money.
- The Breton sweater, with its wide blue-and-white stripes, dates back to the mid-19th century, when it became part of the uniform of the French Navy. In the 1950s and 1960s, it was worn by actors like James Dean, Marlon Brando, and Audrey Hepburn in some of their most famous films, establishing it as a modern fashion staple. Although it was now associated with youth culture and rebelliousness, Lefor-Openo is more likely using it here, for the National Lottery's summer draw, to suggest freedom and the joy of leisure travel.

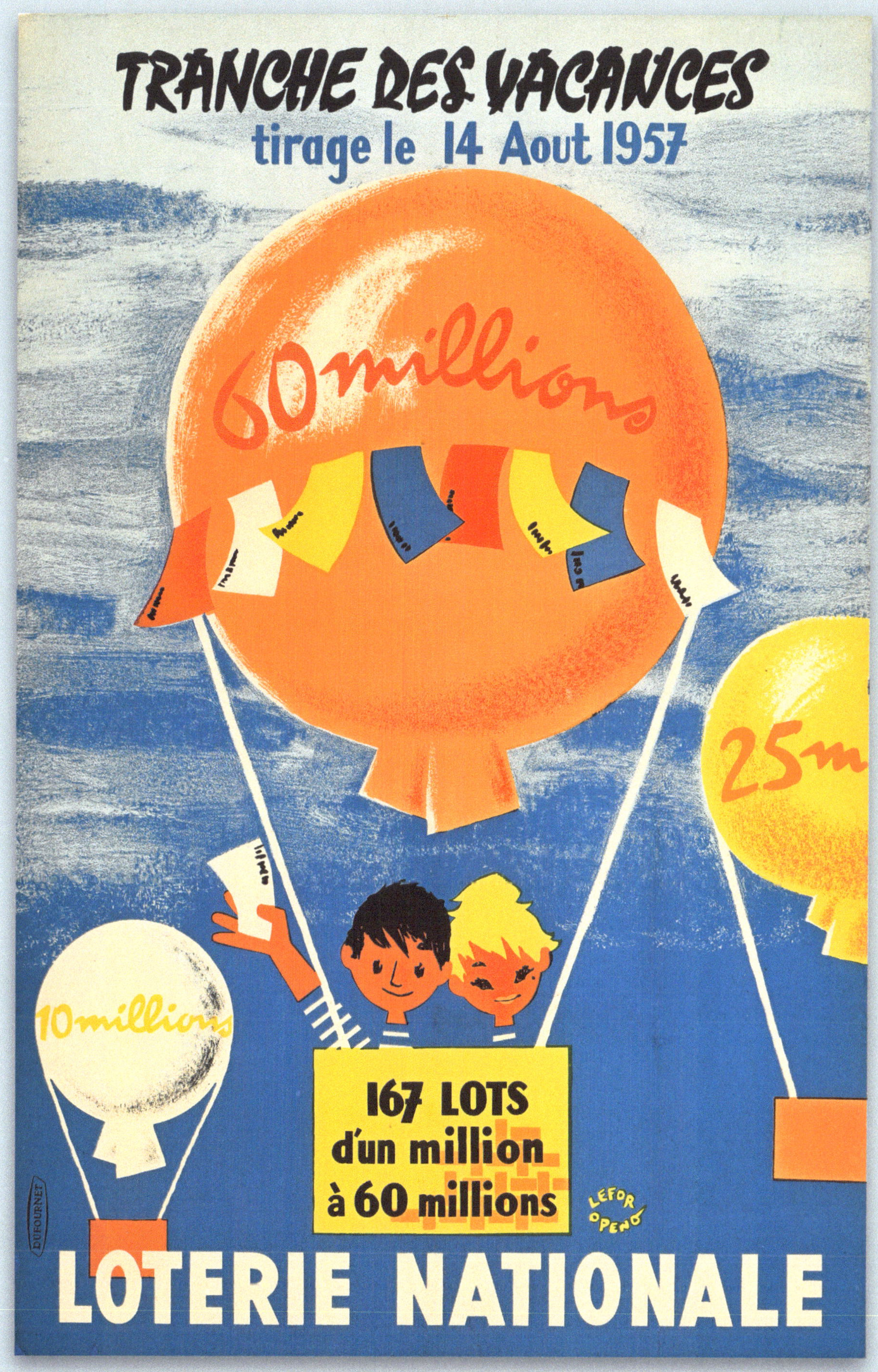
TRANCHE DES VACANCES
tirage le 14 Aout 1957
60 millions
25 m
10 millions
167 LOTS
d'un million
à 60 millions
LEFOR OPENO
DUFOURNET
LOTERIE NATIONALE

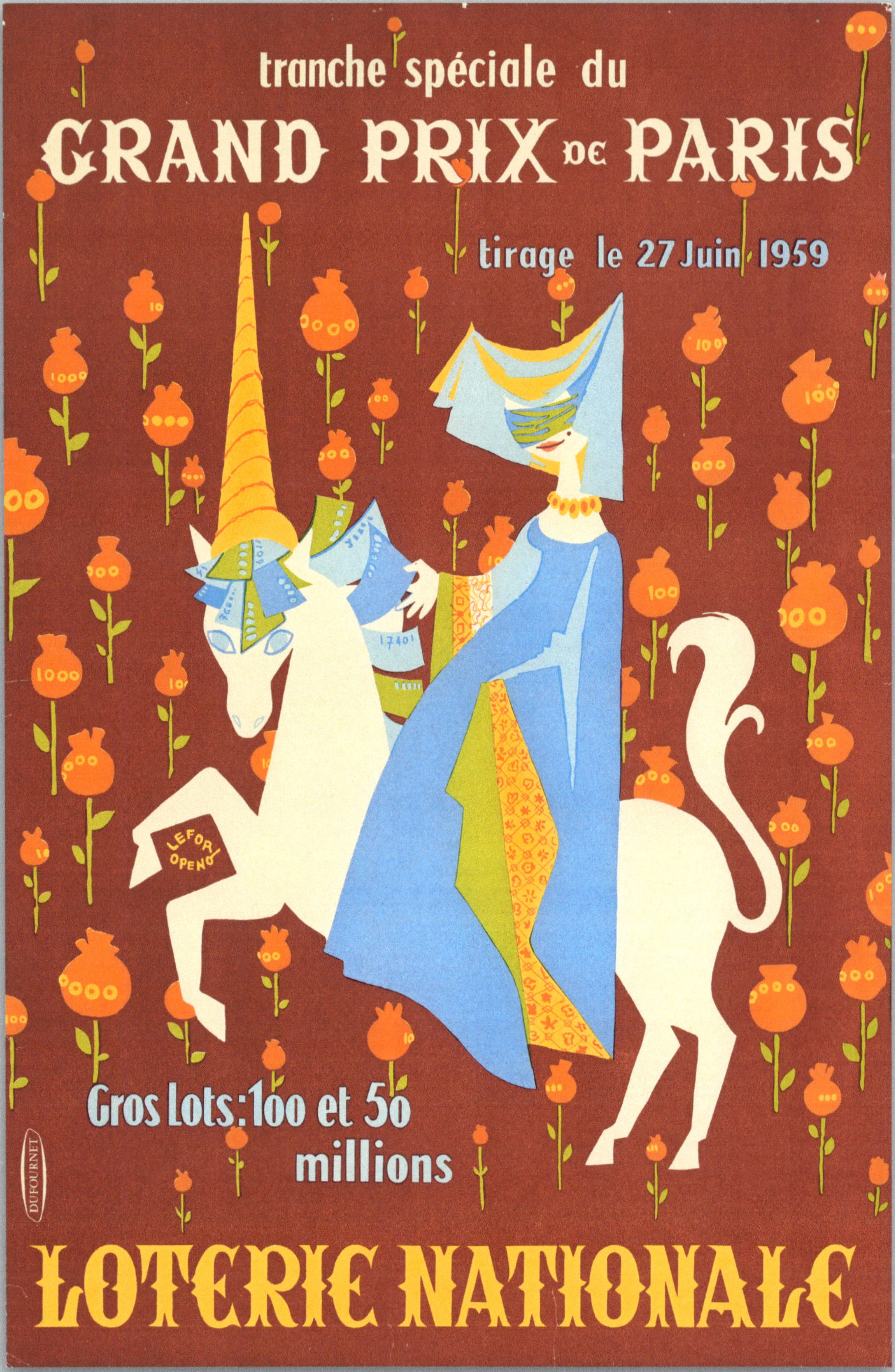

tranche spéciale du

GRAND PRIX DE PARIS

tirage le 27 Juin 1959

LEFOR OPENO

Gros Lots: 100 et 50 millions

DUFOURNET

LOTERIE NATIONALE

Loterie Nationale, 1959

Lefor-Openo (Marie-Claire Lefort, 1931–1971,
and Marie-Francine Oppeneau, 1931–2023)
Poster House Permanent Collection

- *The Lady and the Unicorn* is a series of six tapestries housed in the Musée de Cluny in Paris; they represent the five senses (smell, sight, touch, taste, and sound) along with a sixth sense, "my sole desire." Woven in the early 16th century, this French national treasure is considered an exceptional example of the millefleur style of medieval weaving, in which hundreds of small flowers populate the background of a scene.
- In this interpretation of the story, the buds of the "thousand flowers" are designed as purses of prize money, while the lady, representing blind fortune, rides a unicorn whose horn is a cornucopia overflowing with lottery tickets. The average French citizen would have been familiar enough with the tapestries to know that this scene is intended as an updated version of them.

Loterie Nationale, 1960

Lefor-Openo (Marie-Claire Lefort, 1931–1971, and Marie-Francine Oppeneau, 1931–2023)

Poster House Permanent Collection

- At the end of World War II, France agreed to join the Breton Woods monetary system, which created exchange-rate stability among 44 countries—including the United States, Western Europe, Canada, and Australia—by linking participating countries to the dominant currency of the dollar and the set value of gold. It was developed with the aim of avoiding the financial freefall some countries experienced after World War I, economic crises that produced many of the tensions that ultimately led to a second world war.
- When Charles de Gaulle was elected the president of France in 1958, he inherited an economy that had repeatedly devalued its currency during the preceding decade. As a result of this devaluation, French export prices were naturally lower, and therefore more competitive, for foreign buyers. An increased demand for exported goods also created more domestic jobs, which was essential for French economic recovery after the war. However, many other European countries followed a similar plan, setting up a race to the bottom for who could be the cheapest country with which to do business. This also led to domestic inflation, and French citizens struggled to afford foreign goods.
- In 1959, de Gaulle announced that French currency would be restructured with the introduction of the "new franc," equal to the value of 100 old francs. This was part of a broad plan to prevent further monetary disorder. Its real value, however, was psychological: when someone making a working-class salary can be considered a "millionaire," the international community does not take that economy seriously. As his government was particularly characterized by an obsession with the "grandeur" of France, the new franc therefore served as a powerful symbol of de Gaulle's efforts to reposition the country on the world stage.
- Here, Lefor-Openo adopts the allegorical figure of La Semeuse (the sower), who had first appeared in 1897 on the silver coins of the French Third Republic. She also was featured on de Gaulle's new franc, signifying a return to traditional values and French pride. In this poster, La Semeuse announces that the National Lottery will issue prize money in the new franc, indicated by the letters "NF" on the flowers (they also appeared on overprinted bank notes then in circulation). She remains one of the most enduring symbols of France and was selected to represent the country on French-issued Euro coins in 2002.

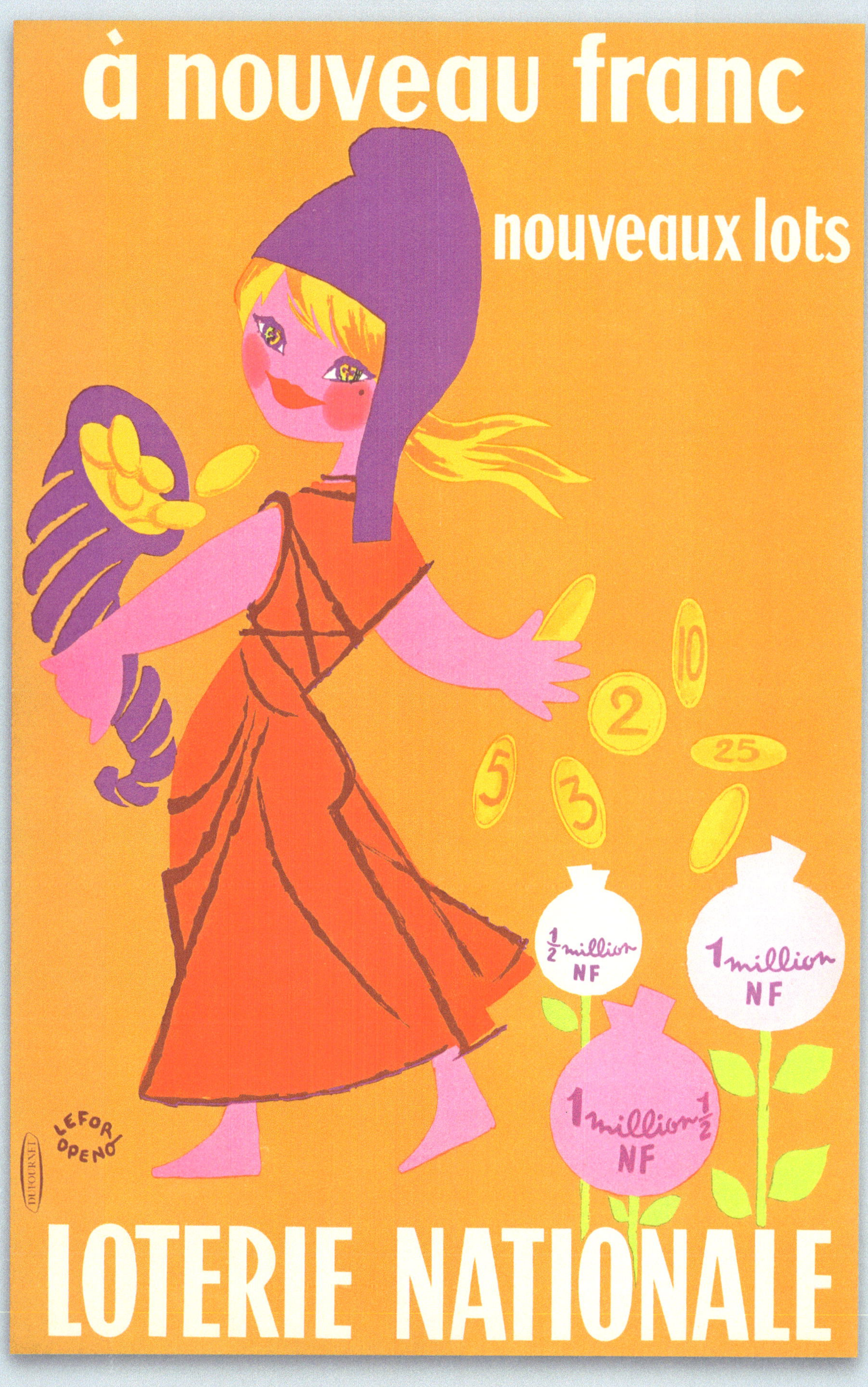

à nouveau franc
nouveaux lots
10
2
25
5
3
½ million NF
1 million NF
1 million ½ NF
LEFOR OPENO
DUFOURNET
LOTERIE NATIONALE

LOTERIE NATIONALE

double CHANCE

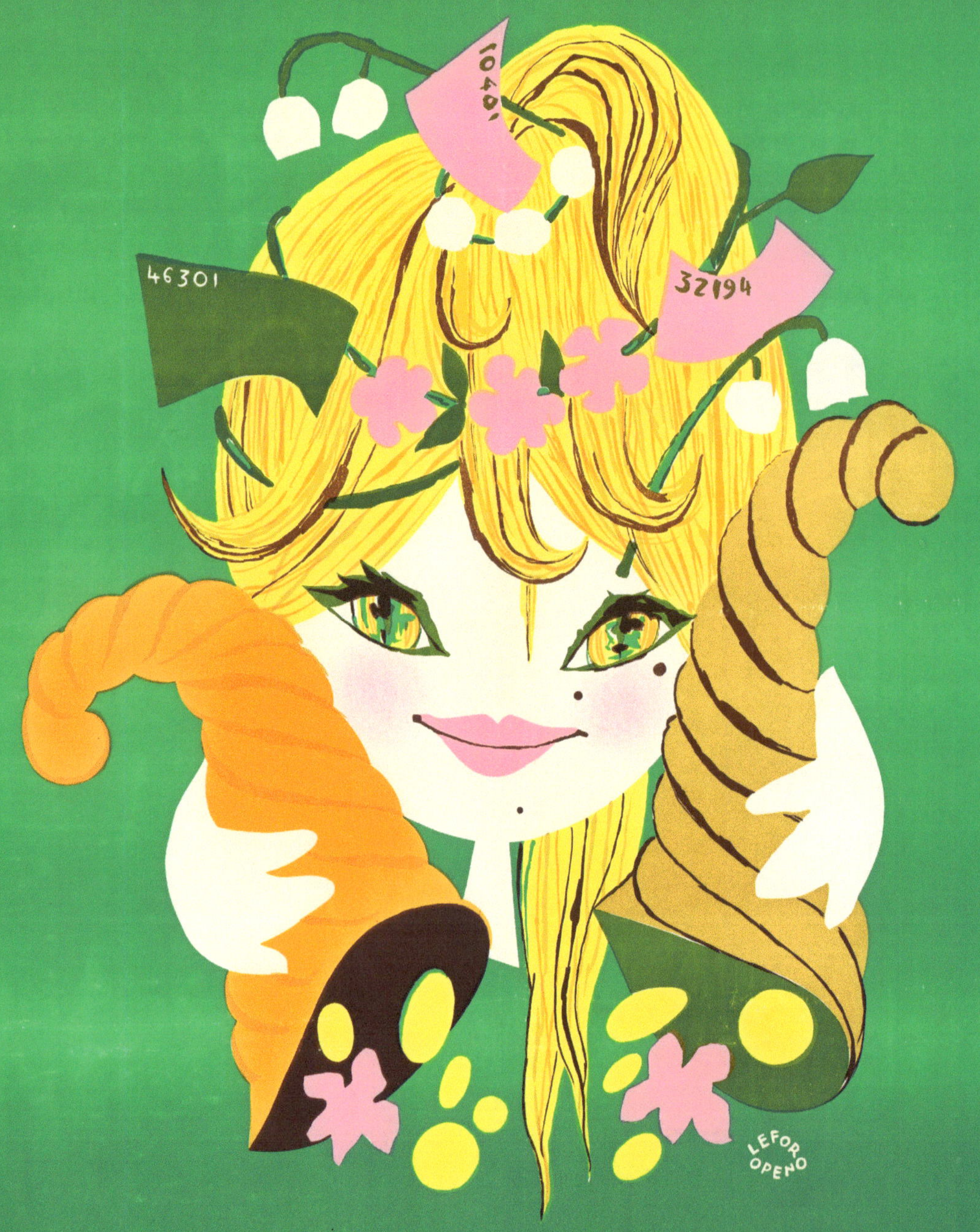

DUFOURNET
74, rue Blanche Paris 9e

TIRAGE LE 18 MAI 1960

deux gros lots de 1 million NF

Imp RUSSEL . PARIS

Loterie Nationale, 1960

Lefor-Openo (Marie-Claire Lefort, 1931–1971, and Marie-Francine Oppeneau, 1931–2023)

Poster House Permanent Collection

- National Lottery tickets were primarily sold by war widows stationed in small booths on the street. Posters promoting that week's draw were commonly pasted on the front or sides of these booths, meaning that most had to be printed in small formats. Larger-format posters like this one are less common and would have been displayed in designated outdoor advertising spaces throughout Paris.
- This design features the mature version of the signature female figure that launched Lefor-Openo into the national consciousness. Based on the actress Brigitte Bardot, her joyful, cartoonish face is characterized by wide eyes, a broad mouth, a trendy *choucroute* hairstyle (blonde beehive with curls), rosy cheeks, and a small beauty mark (known in French as a *mouche* or "fly") under her left eye. She appeared in endless iterations throughout Lefor-Openo's career, selling everything from lottery tickets to soft drinks.
- The public responded so positively to this type of cutesy imagery that Lefor-Openo soon had numerous imitators; the most prominent of these was Alain Gauthier, who adopted a similar coquettish young woman in his posters. This saturation of advertising with flirtatious womanhood reflected a collective French preoccupation with a particular type of girlish femininity.
- In 1969, nearly a decade after Lefor-Openo chose Bardot as the inspiration for their advertising hallmark, the actress was selected to be the first official face of Marianne (the personification of the French Republic since the Revolution) and temporarily became the internationally recognized symbol of Liberty for France.

THE RETURN OF DE GAULLE

Soon after Nazi Germany began its occupation of France in June 1940, the Vichy Government was established to run the southern, "unoccupied" part of the country; in November 1942, the Germans moved into that region, and Vichy became a puppet regime. While officially neutral, it collaborated with the Nazis, instituted a repressive authoritarian state, enacted antisemitic racial laws, and deported many Jewish citizens to extermination camps. Meanwhile, General Charles de Gaulle assumed the leadership role for the French Resistance from his government-in-exile in London, instructing rebel cells and military officials from afar. After the Liberation of France in August 1944, de Gaulle became the head of the Provisional Government of the French Republic, an interim leadership for the country until France adopted a new constitution in October 1946, creating the Fourth Republic. de Gaulle did not approve of the limitations of the new constitution and resigned a few months later, retiring from politics entirely in 1953.

The Fourth Republic proved politically unstable, undergoing 21 different administrations in a 12-year period. While the economy and living standards for French citizens improved during this time, confidence in the government diminished, especially against the backdrop of the French war in Indochina (present-day Vietnam, Laos, and Cambodia), which resulted in France losing its colonies in the region in 1954. In May of that year, civil unrest broke out in the much-closer country of Algeria, home to more than a million French citizens. By 1958, this conflict had escalated, further undermining public confidence in the Fourth Republic. Members of the French army and some European settlers staged a military coup in Algiers, demanding that de Gaulle return to power to restore order to France and prevent Algeria from gaining independence. On May 15, de Gaulle publicly agreed to take charge on the condition that he was given full legislative authority and the ability to rewrite the constitution. He did not mention his plans for Algeria.

The posters produced by Lefor-Openo during this period are inherently political; however, the few records that survive indicate that neither member of the team necessarily agreed with or opposed the messaging in these designs—the commissions were a job, and their sole goal was to produce quality work.

Rente 3.5%, 1958

Lefor-Openo (Marie-Claire Lefort, 1931–1971, and Marie-Francine Oppeneau, 1931–2023)

Poster House Permanent Collection

- On June 3, 1958, de Gaulle was given a six-month period of investiture by the National Assembly, during which time he was expected to bring stability to France. In order to fund his ambitious plans, he needed a large influx of capital; however, the Bank of France was in a precarious position, with a deeply devalued currency. de Gaulle appointed Antoine Pinay as his minister of finance, a role Pinay had also held while he was prime minister between March and December 1952.
- During Pinay's original term in office, which was also marked by financial instability and inflation, he had spearheaded what would later become known as the Pinay Loan, a bond tied to the fixed price of gold that would yield a 3.5 percent annual return. Profits were exempt from both income and inheritance taxes, and anyone who brought in money from outside the country to invest in this bond was offered a tax amnesty (many wealthy Europeans kept their money in offshore accounts to avoid taxes and because they lacked confidence in the stability of the French banking system). The bond was overwhelmingly successful, bringing in 428 billion francs to the state and helping to temporarily stabilize the economy.
- de Gaulle asked Pinay to try the same idea again in 1958 and went on national television to endorse the bond program, speaking of its past success and the country's need for public support.
- Pinay himself chose Lefor-Openo's design to announce the bond; it features a serene Marianne knitting a sock out of gold thread—a physical representation of a "bas de laine" (woolen stocking, a French expression for "nest egg" or the treasure one keeps at home). The poster was displayed in a variety of sizes all over the country between June 17 and July 12, and it ultimately raised 324 billion francs. Mentioned in numerous press articles, it became the symbol of a new political stability and a breakout moment for the two designers—who were now part of the face of a new France.

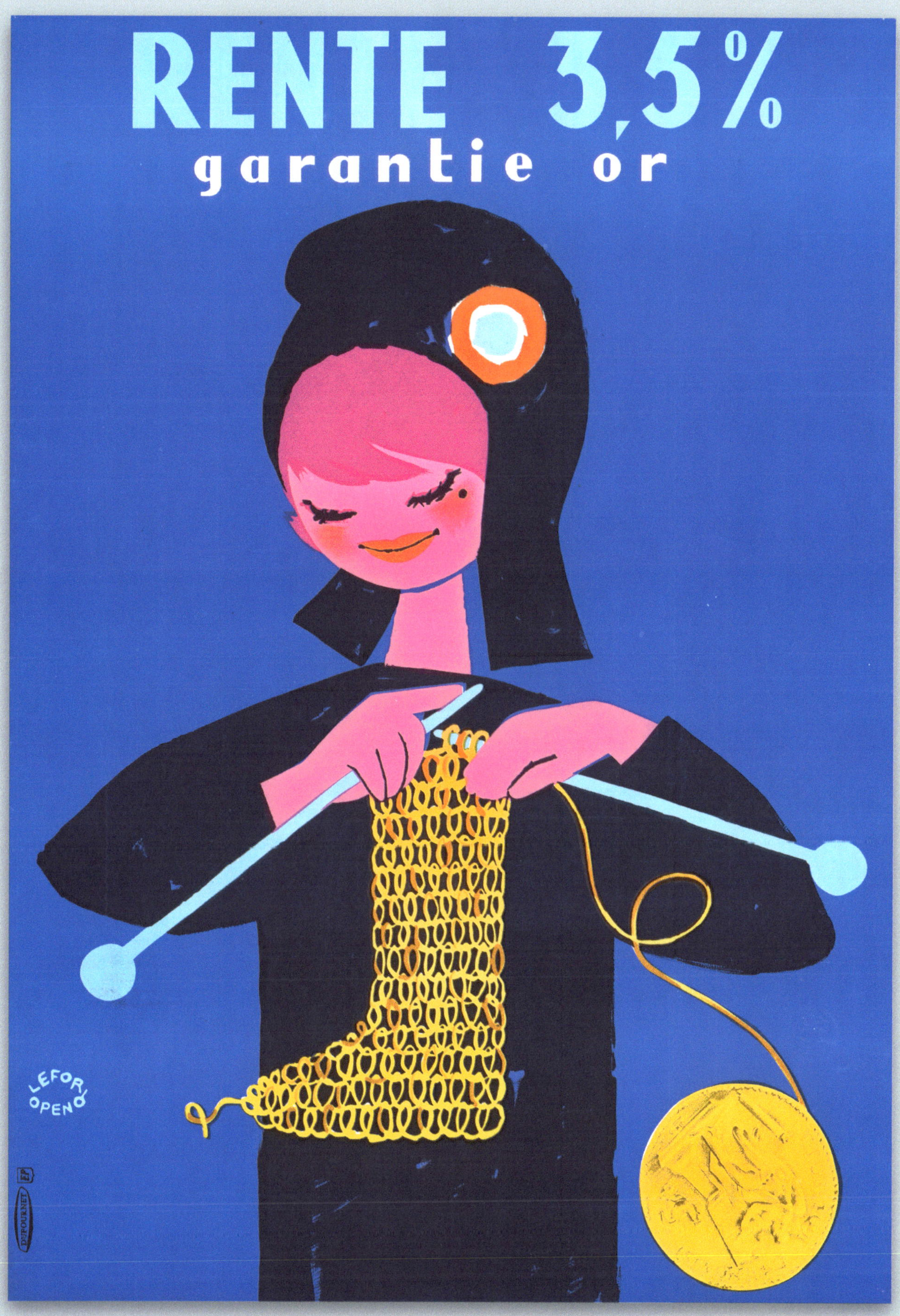

RENTE 3,5%
garantie or
LEFOR OPENO

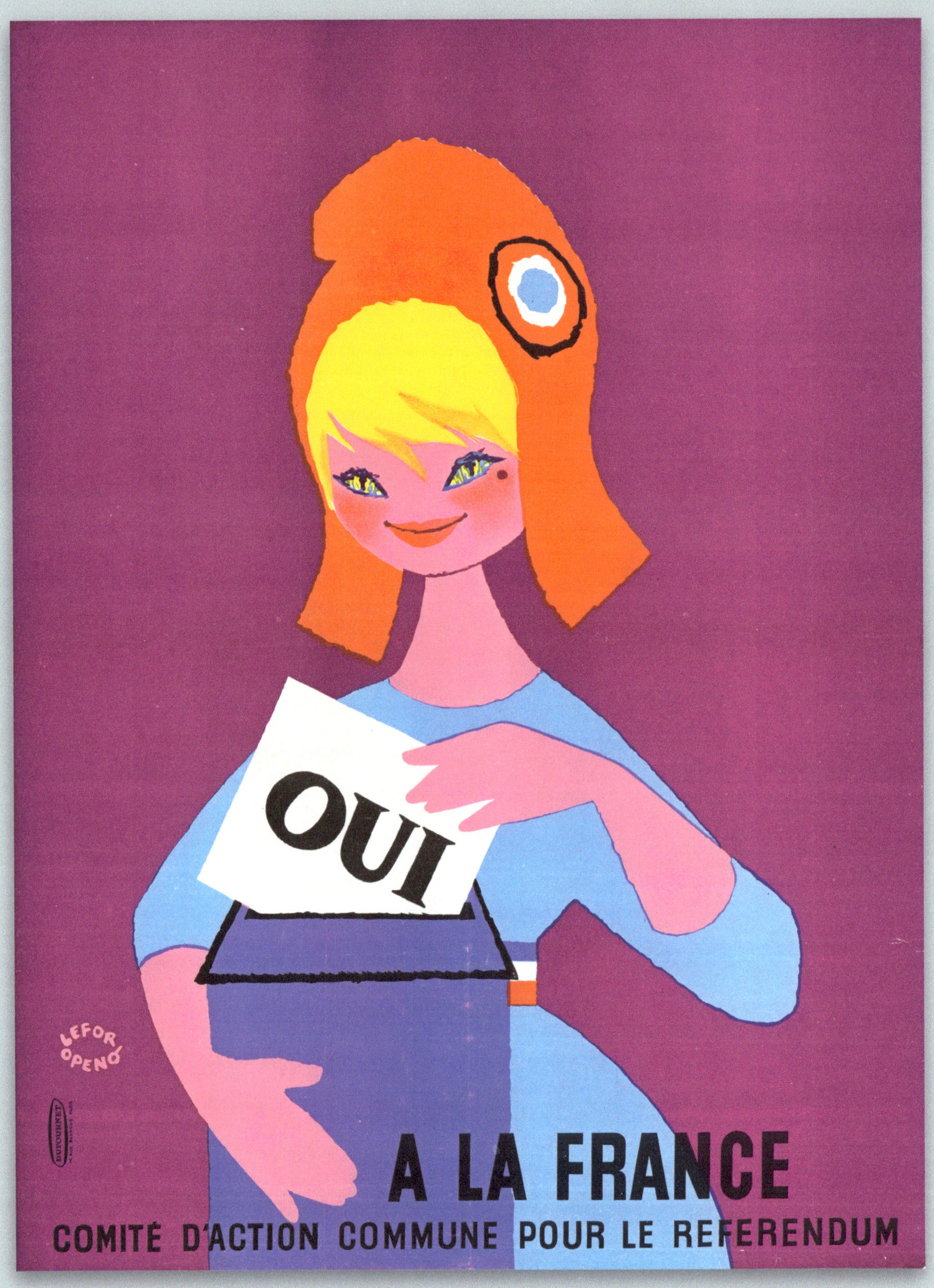
OUI
LEFOR OPENO
A LA FRANCE
COMITÉ D'ACTION COMMUNE POUR LE REFERENDUM

Oui à la France, 1958

Lefor-Openo (Marie-Claire Lefort, 1931–1971,
and Marie-Francine Oppeneau, 1931–2023)
Poster House Permanent Collection

- Four months into his temporary position as the absolute leader of France, Charles de Gaulle held a referendum: French citizens were asked to vote to approve a new constitution, thereby dissolving the Fourth Republic and creating the Fifth.
- The current constitution had only existed since 1946; this updated version expanded the power of the presidency (which had previously been mainly ceremonial) so that he now had the sole authority to appoint a prime minister as well as the ability to dissolve the National Assembly and take on full governmental power in "exceptional circumstances." Parliament lost much of its power, leading to fewer checks and balances at the executive branch.
- In addition to domestic changes, the new constitution asked all outlying French territories and colonies if they wished to gain immediate independence or have their own autonomous governments within the French community. The only territory to vote against remaining within France's orbit was Guinea, which gained its independence within a few days of the vote.
- Focusing on a woman casting her vote in the referendum was a strategic choice for this campaign. Women had only recently gained the right to vote and were approximately 12 percent more likely to abstain from participating than men, but also 9 percent more inclined to vote for a conservative candidate like de Gaulle. By making a vote in favor of the new constitution the clear choice for women, Lefor-Openo helped secure de Gaulle's desired result.

Dites Oui, 1958

Lefor-Openo (Marie-Claire Lefort, 1931–1971, and Marie-Francine Oppeneau, 1931–2023)

Poster House Permanent Collection

- This and the companion design by Lefor-Openo used to promote voting in favor of de Gaulle's new constitution were selected by André Malraux, a notable French novelist who also became the country's first minister of cultural affairs. The images were printed in runs of more than 200,000 copies and pasted throughout France. The press noted the particular impact of these posters, which appear to have encouraged the overwhelming 82.6 percent who voted in favor of ratifying the new constitution on September 28, 1958.
- In 1944, Charles de Gaulle's interim government granted women the right to vote. It was one of the last European countries to provide universal suffrage. Despite this achievement, women were still treated as second-class citizens, unable to seek employment or have their own bank accounts without their husbands' permission. In addition, married women did not have control over their own property or any rights to their children; they could not file for divorce without provable cause (and even then, not until they had been married for at least three years), nor could they choose where they lived. Contraception and abortion were also illegal.
- This image presents a young woman agreeing to "marry" the new France (and, by extension, de Gaulle), a patriotic duty emphasized by the red, white, and blue bouquet and rosette on her Phrygian cap (a symbol of the French Republic). Even the language ("say yes") is reminiscent of the "I do" in traditional marriage vows. Such design choices underscore the paternalistic overtones of de Gaulle's government and the larger male-centric social structure of France in the 1950s, one in which women were primarily valued as wives and mothers. The majority of French women at this time would not have found this distasteful, but as an assertion of the sacred role of their gender in ensuring a prosperous future for France.

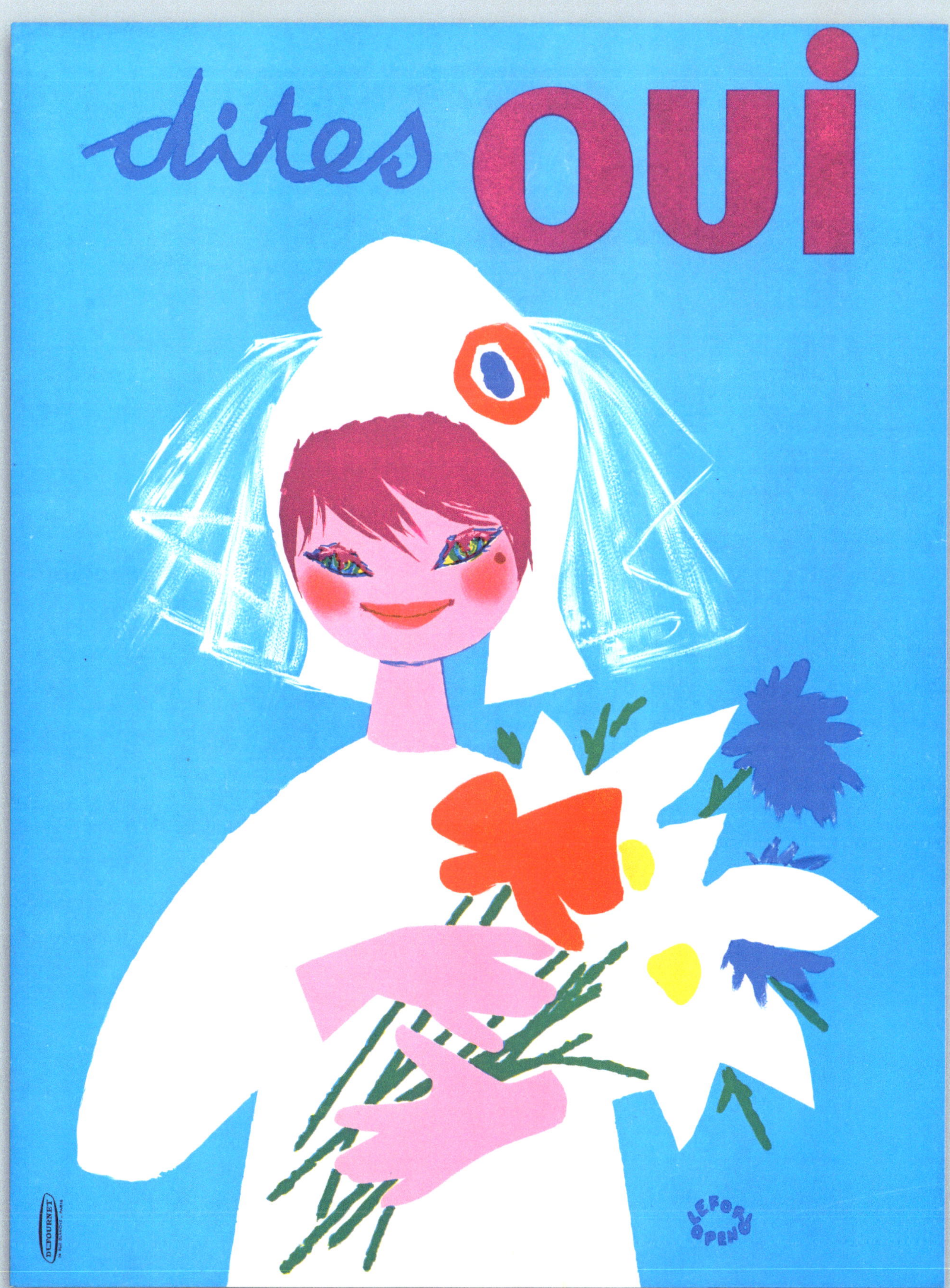
dites OUI
LEFOR OPENO
DUFOURNET

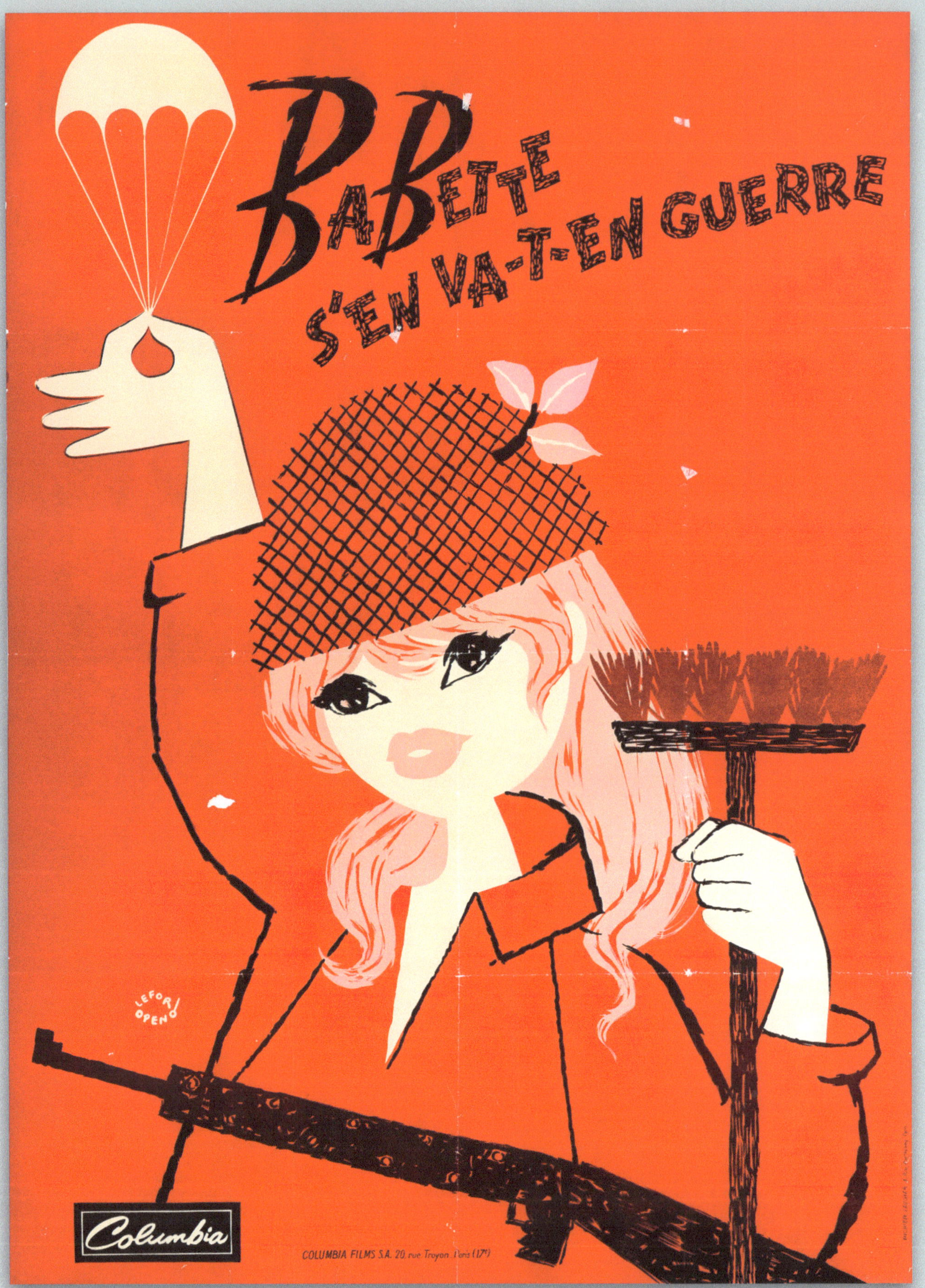
BABETTE
S'EN VA-T-EN GUERRE
LEFOR OPENO
Columbia
COLUMBIA FILMS S.A. 20, rue Troyon Paris (17e)

Babette s'en va-t-en Guerre, 1959

Lefor-Openo (Marie-Claire Lefort, 1931–1971, and Marie-Francine Oppeneau, 1931–2023)

Poster House Permanent Collection

- *Babette Goes to War* is a wartime comedy chronicling the misadventures of a French housekeeper who parachutes into German-occupied France to thwart the Nazis and help win the war. While not an overt piece of pro–de Gaulle propaganda, the release of a film during his presidency that reminded audiences of the importance of the French Resistance that he had once led reinforced his positive public image. de Gaulle himself was a fan of the film's star, Brigitte Bardot, insisting that her contribution to the French economy was equal to that of Renault, the country's most exported automobile.
- The director of the film, Raoul Lévy, approached Lefor-Openo with the request to create this poster because of the striking resemblance between the star and their signature character in the referendum poster the year before. The designers had already told the press that they had been inspired by Bardot as well as by the general aesthetic of contemporary young women who emulated her.
- Bardot was a complex figure within French female identity. She typically played innocent characters (orphans, schoolgirls) who were oblivious to their hypersexualization within a film's narrative. These movies most often end with her marrying a more worldly, fatherlike figure, thereby making her an "acceptable" French woman—one ready for her duty as a wife and mother. Even her nickname, "B.B." (*bébé* or baby), which is graphically emphasized in the poster, implies a need for paternal protection.
- This poster was pivotal in Lefor-Openo's career because it introduced them to an international audience: most posters for the foreign release of the film, which was widely distributed and became one of the highest-grossing movies of the year, featured a variation of this image. Even in posters that relied on photography rather than illustration, a mini Lefor-Openo Bardot was present somewhere in the design. This poster for the French release was printed in three colors (patriotic red, white, and blue) and often pasted along streets in rows to evoke the country's flag.

Oui A Notre Avenir, c. 1965

Lefor-Openo (Marie-Claire Lefort, 1931–1971, and Marie-Francine Oppeneau, 1931–2023)

Poster House Permanent Collection

- While still featuring the silhouette of a woman in a Phrygian cap, this design by Lefor-Openo is far more pared down than their typical compositions. It recalls numerous generic posters, printed by the government during the lead-up to the vote on the 1958 referendum, that incorporated traditional symbols of France as visual shorthand for de Gaulle.
- The poster advertises the Women's Center for Studies and Information, a Gaullist organization founded in 1965 with the goal of educating and supporting women to participate in the "civic, economic, social, and cultural life of France." While it promoted many modern feminist ideas, it also adhered to the national belief that a woman's primary duty is to be a mother and preserve the family unit.
- Produced around the time of the first direct presidential election in which de Gaulle was a candidate, this is likely a campaign poster for him masquerading as something else. In France, each candidate is allocated the same amount of dedicated outdoor space for political advertisements. These panels are typically placed outside of polling stations to influence and inform voters. Political posters displayed elsewhere would be removed by the police. A poster like this one does not appear to promote any specific candidate and, therefore, there was little risk of it being automatically taken down; however, any viewer at the time would have recognized the imagery as clearly Gaullist.

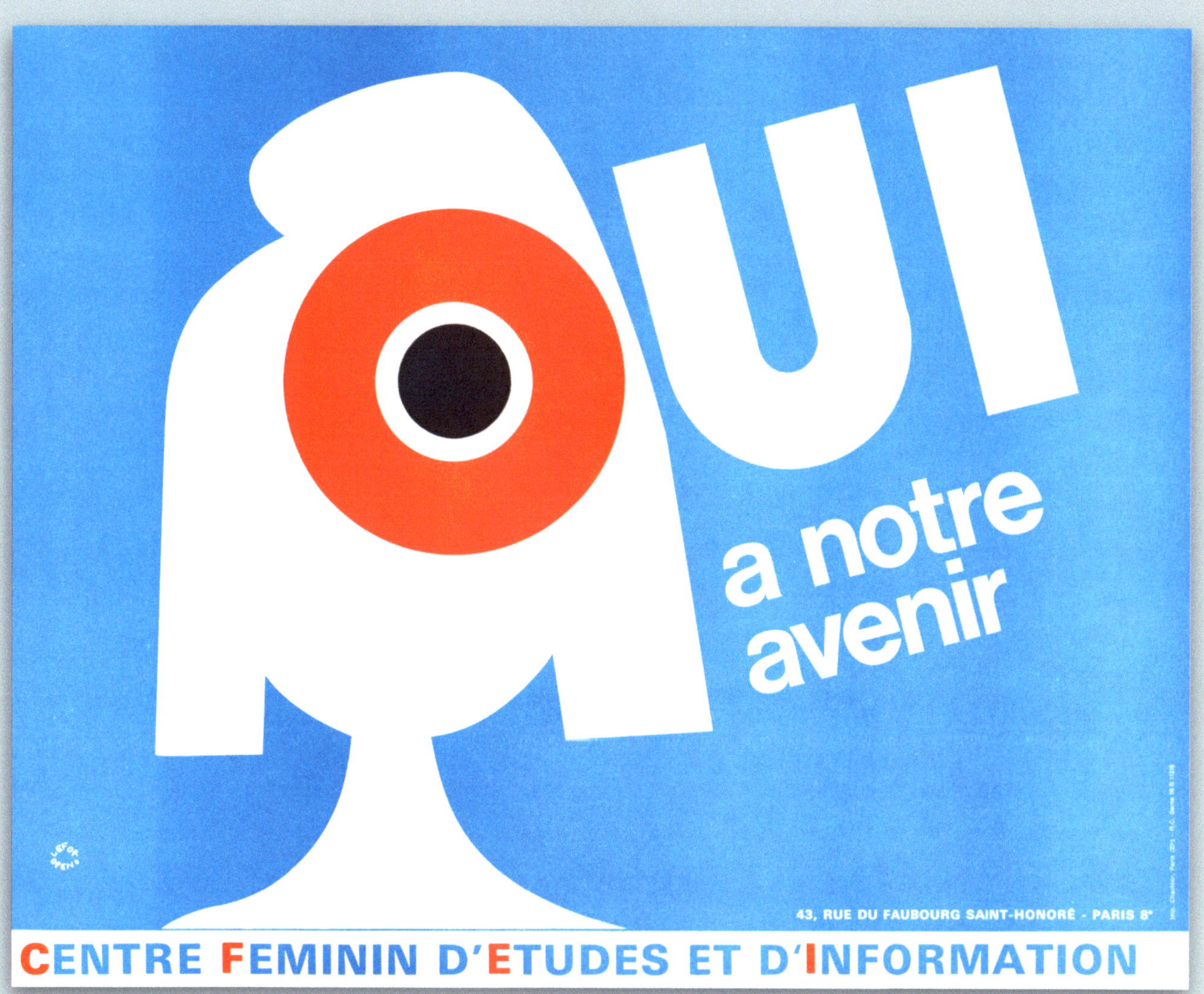
OUI
a notre
avenir
43, RUE DU FAUBOURG SAINT-HONORÉ - PARIS 8e
CENTRE FEMININ D'ETUDES ET D'INFORMATION

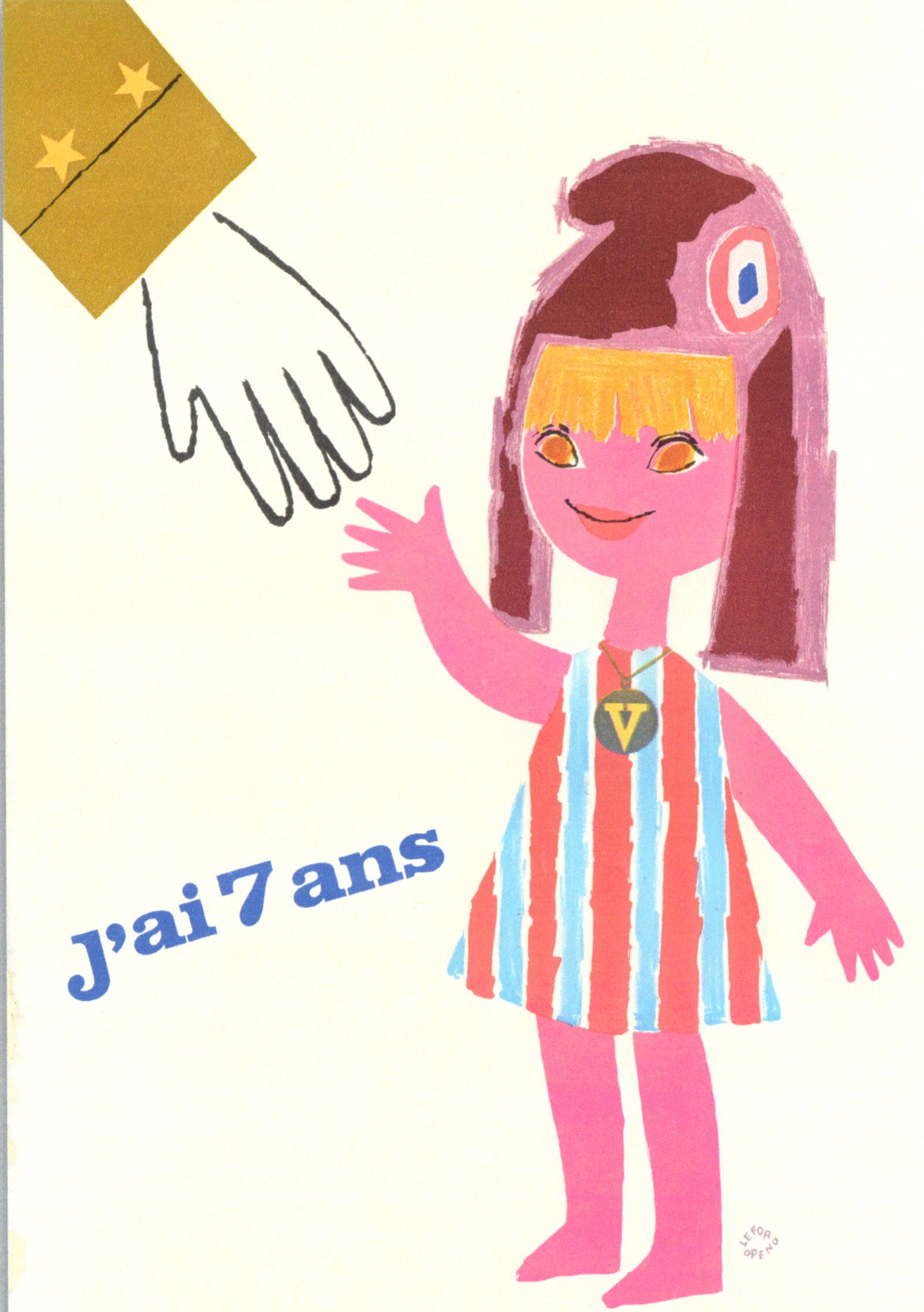

laissez-moi grandir

Imp. S. A. COURBET, Paris

Laissez-Moi Grandir, 1965

Lefor-Openo (Marie-Claire Lefort, 1931–1971, and Marie-Francine Oppeneau, 1931–2023)

Poster House Permanent Collection

- Three years before he was up for reelection, Charles de Gaulle amended the constitution to allow the president to be elected by direct universal suffrage rather than by an electoral college. The 1965 election advertised in this poster would be the first to adhere to this new system.
- As they had done for the 1958 referendum, Lefor-Openo created two designs, the first of which features a young girl wearing multiple patriotic symbols: a dress made up of the French tricolor, the Phrygian cap with the tricolor cockade (representing Liberty), and a badge with the V for Victory. She is reaching for the hand of de Gaulle himself (indicated by the starred cuff of his military uniform). Combined with the tagline "I am seven years old; let me grow up," she stands in for the Fifth Republic as it asks de Gaulle to guide it through adolescence and provide the stability of a father figure.
- The tagline can also be interpreted as a disclaimer against any missteps that occurred during the first few years of the Fifth Republic. As a young government structure, mistakes were bound to be made, and the poster requests public tolerance for such growing pains.
- While de Gaulle was considered likely to be reelected, the requirement that he receive a majority vote led to a second-round runoff between him and François Mitterrand, a left-wing politician who would become France's longest-serving president in the 1980s and 1990s. de Gaulle ultimately won the election with a margin of more than 2 million votes.

Confiance en la France/Confiance en De Gaulle, 1965

Lefor-Openo (Marie-Claire Lefort, 1931–1971,
and Marie-Francine Oppeneau, 1931–2023)
Poster House Permanent Collection

- Also created for the 1965 presidential election, this poster is a significant departure from Lefor-Openo's typical output. More painterly than graphic, it shares an affinity with the work of popular French painter Bernard Buffet, who had been commissioned by *TIME* magazine in 1958 to produce a portrait of de Gaulle for its cover announcing him as "Man of the Year." Lefor-Openo would have been familiar with this portrait and might have been inspired by it when creating this composition.
- The image shows a Marianne figure wearing various symbols of France next to the Cross of Lorraine, a 16th-century symbol adopted by the French Resistance during World War II. It became deeply associated with de Gaulle and was used by many of the conservative political groups that supported him. Here, the cross is adorned with small leaves, indicating, as in the other poster, that the young Fifth Republic still needs nurturing.
- The accompanying text was used on a variety of political posters during the election and urges voters to "Trust in France, Trust in de Gaulle."

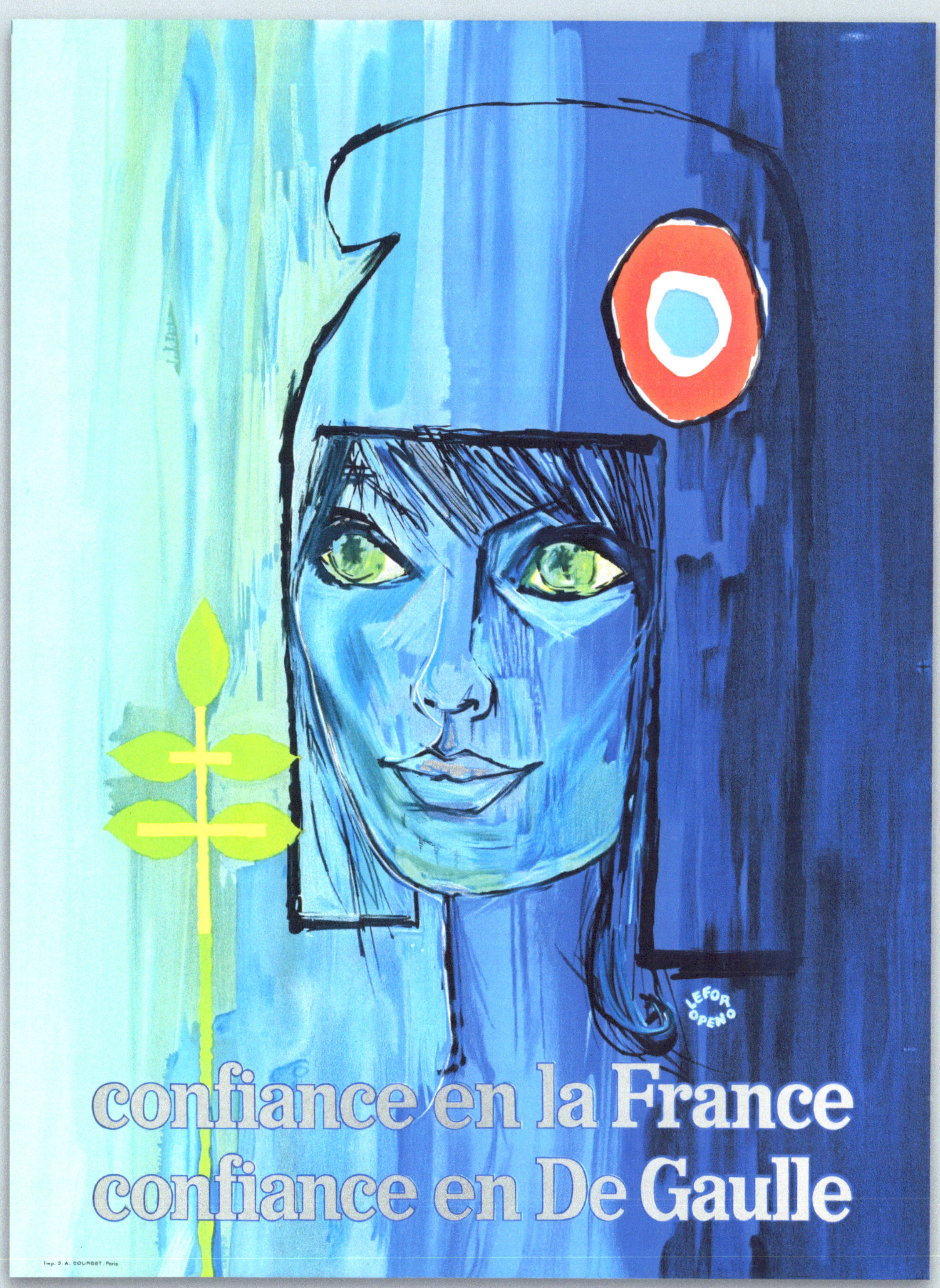
LEFOR OPENO
confiance en la France
confiance en De Gaulle
Imp. S.A. COURBET. Paris

A SINGULAR CHAPTER IN FRENCH POSTER DESIGN (1955–1967)

THE WORK OF MARIE-CLAIRE LEFORT AND MARIE-FRANCINE OPPENEAU

Vincent Joigneaux

The uniqueness of the Lefor-Openo design team lies first and foremost in the fact that it comprised two young women working together in an artistic partnership, a situation that was highly unusual in the context of French poster design of the 1950s and 1960s. At a time when poster designers were overwhelmingly male, and when this kind of collaboration was rare, the work of the pair immediately attracted the attention of publishers, advertisers, and the specialized press; this, in turn, played a decisive role in their rapid and spectacular rise to prominence.

Marie-Claire Lefort (1932–1971) and Marie-Francine Oppeneau (1932–2023) were quick to recognize and capitalize on this exceptional position. They were keenly attuned to the expectations of their clients as well as to those of the general public, developing a style that was immediately recognizable, one that combined graphic efficiency with a sensitivity to contemporary social codes. Their work is thus deeply rooted in the society of postwar France and the decades of economic growth known as *Les Trente Glorieuses* (The Thirty Glorious Years), and it remains a valuable record of that era.

TRAINING AND THE BIRTH OF A BRAND

Both born in 1932 from middle-class backgrounds, Marie-Claire Lefort and Marie-Francine Oppeneau met in 1950, shortly after completing their secondary education at the Lycée Claude-Bernard in Paris. There, they studied drawing as they prepared for careers in teaching. At the end of their three-year program, however, they both decided to seek a more independent and experimental form of artistic training.

Lefort and Oppeneau enrolled at the École Paul Colin, the school founded by the renowned painter and poster designer whose career had flourished since the 1920s. More than a conventional educational institution, Colin's school functioned as an open and lively workshop, welcoming aspiring decorators and advertising designers. Colin himself focused on the individual talents of the students, encouraging them to follow distinctive and personal artistic paths. Although Lefort and Oppeneau initially dreamed of designing stage sets for the theater, Colin urged them to explore poster design—and to do so together.

Thus, at the age of 23, they entered the world of advertising under the name "Lefor-Openo," a contraction of their surnames. This shared signature would soon become a recognizable and original brand.

EARLY COMMISSIONS AND PROFESSIONAL RECOGNITION

By virtue of their social milieu and a network of personal connections, Lefor-Openo quickly secured their first commissions, most notably posters for balls organized by the prestigious *grandes écoles* (specialized universities operating outside the public university system in France). In addition, Marie-Claire Lefort's father's role as a member of the city council in Vichy enabled the designers to obtain numerous local commissions, including promotional posters for the town, the casino, and the theater.

The year 1955 marked a decisive turning point for Lefor-Openo. They won the prize for the official poster of the 46th Concours Lépine, a major national inventors' contest; this award gave them unprecedented visibility and attracted even more attention from the press. That same year, they produced their first poster for the Loterie Nationale (National Lottery). Their success was immediate and lasting: the organization would regularly commission work from them until 1960.

THE CREATION OF AN ARCHETYPAL CHARACTER

Around 1957 or 1958, Lefor-Openo designed what would become the hallmark of their work: A stylized female figure, halfway between children's illustration and gentle caricature. With her round face, cheerful smile, fashionable hairstyle, full skirt, and often a small beauty mark beneath her eye, this young woman was distinguished by her simplicity, charm, and contagious optimism.

The character embodied an appealing image of modern womanhood: a fulfilled, smiling housewife who fully embraced the promises offered by postwar consumer society. In scenes imbued with a light, benevolent humor, Lefor-Openo presented a reassuring and attractive vision of contemporary domesticity. Their approach perfectly met advertisers' expectations while resonating with a broad audience.

The two designers, themselves both young and well aware of trends in fashion and social behavior, intuitively captured the spirit of their time. Their character became a kind of mascot—an idealized representation of the young French woman of the late 1950s and, in many respects, of her creators themselves.

NATIONAL RECOGNITION AND PUBLIC VISIBILITY

In 1958, Lefor-Openo were at the very forefront of the French graphic design scene. That year, they designed the poster promoting the new Pinay government loan in June, followed by two different posters for the September referendum that established the Fifth Republic. Printed in several hundred thousand copies, these posters were displayed in towns and villages throughout France. The designers' signature style became instantly recognizable, and their reputation was firmly established.

This visibility soon led to more important commissions. A film producer approached them to design the poster for a new film, *Babette s'en va-t-en guerre* (Babette Goes to War), starring Brigitte Bardot. The choice was particularly apt; although she was not a literal image of the actress, the classic Lefor-Openo character clearly reflected

Bardot's decisive influence on the appearance, clothing, and hairstyles of young women at the time.

That same year, the national electricity company Électricité de France (EDF) enlisted the pair's services for a collaboration that would last until 1967. Lefor-Openo produced numerous posters promoting such household appliances as electric water heaters, washing machines, cookers, and refrigerators. This body of work powerfully associated them with domestic modernity and technological progress, even if such a connection hardly did justice to the full range of their creative output.

In 1959, a journalist famously referred to Lefor-Openo as "state poster designers," a paradoxical label for two young women deeply committed to independence, yet one that underscored their prominent role in institutional communication during this period.

BETWEEN SUCCESS AND CONFINEMENT

Celebrated for their ability to depict the modern housewife from a female perspective, Lefor-Openo were increasingly sought after by private companies, particularly in the household-appliance sector. Advertisers often insisted that they include in these new posters the female figure that had made the team famous.

While poster design traditionally relies on a central idea or concept, in the case of Lefor-Openo it was the character itself that gave the product its identity. This specificity ultimately proved to be both an asset and a constraint. Gradually, the designers found themselves confined by the very formula that had determined their success.

In the early 1960s, however, a wider range of commissions allowed them to expand their repertoire to some extent. They created posters for the cigarette brand Gitanes, and between 1960 and 1962 they worked for the footwear company Bata and for Eastman Kodak Company. During this period, their emblematic character was allowed certain variations and was sometimes integrated into a broader family setting, signaling an effort to evolve and diversify.

In 1965, two of Lefor-Openo's designs that differed markedly from their usual style were selected for General de Gaulle's presidential campaign. One featured a naive, childlike figure; the other depicted an adult Marianne, rendered in a spare, linear style reminiscent of the work of the Expressionist painter and printmaker Bernard Buffet. These works testify to Lefor-Openo's ability to adapt to more symbolic and solemn registers.

NEW DIRECTIONS

By the late 1960s, Lefor-Openo had begun to distance themselves from poster design. A 1966 exhibition of their personal paintings (held in the rue de Bourgogne in Paris) was simply titled "Lefor-Openo" and points to this gradual move away from graphic design, one motivated partly by changes in their personal lives, not the least of which was the birth of their children.

More broadly, they felt increasingly out of step with the field itself. Poster design was increasingly dominated by photographic imagery and was now largely commissioned by agencies. As independent designers, Lefor-Openo were ill-prepared for these developments, and their style—closely associated with the previous decade—was, in any case, much less in demand.

In 1970, the women opened an art gallery in Saint-Cloud in the western suburbs of Paris, marking a new chapter in their professional lives. This venture came to an abrupt end when Marie-Claire Lefort experienced serious health issues. Without her partner, Marie-Francine Oppeneau definitively turned away from poster design.

Until her death in 2023, however, Oppeneau continued to use the name Lefor-Openo in her work as a gallery owner, a gesture of loyalty to her friend and collaborator. Their shared career remains a rare and significant professional adventure—one that is inseparable from the social and cultural transformations of postwar France—and their work stands today as a vivid visual testament to a distant era of social and economic optimism.

ELECTRICITY AND THE MODERN HOUSEWIFE

Established in 1946 during Charles de Gaulle's interim government, Électricité de France (EDF) was the result of a postwar effort to consolidate and strengthen a fragmented electrical grid system, taking the country's electricity management away from approximately 1,700 private companies and merging them under a single, government-run organization. While its first order of business was rebuilding the electrical network that had been severely damaged during the war, by the time de Gaulle was in power again in 1958, it was able to focus on one of the major tenets of his vision for the future of France: self-sufficiency.

After the Suez Crisis in 1956, during which many European countries were constrained due to their reliance on foreign oil and the dominance of the United States in international foreign policy, de Gaulle asserted that energy independence was essential for the future of France—especially given that the country's energy consumption had more than doubled in the past decade. He pursued an ambitious assortment of projects to achieve this goal, including the construction of the Serre-Ponçon Dam and, eventually, a series of French-made nuclear reactors. If France did not have to import energy, electricity would remain relatively inexpensive for the population even if the franc depreciated in value.

While most French households were connected to the national grid by the mid-1950s, many citizens maintained habits from the early postwar period when electricity was rationed. They were also still getting used to the increased incomes and quality of life associated with the economic boom of the 1950s and needed encouragement to purchase the many time-saving appliances that were becoming affordable to the growing middle class. In 1954, Crédit Cetelem en ligne (CETELEM) became the first consumer credit program in France that allowed individuals to purchase appliances through loans. Starting in 1957, EDF launched an aggressive campaign in specific regions of the country to see if advertising would impact consumer habits over a four-year period. Combined, these efforts resulted in a dramatic increase in consumer spending on both household appliances and electricity usage. Of the hundreds of posters that supported these programs, Lefor-Openo's were especially notable, setting the tone for the modern French family and the prescribed role women played within it.

L'eau chaude Électrique, 1958

Lefor-Openo (Marie-Claire Lefort, 1931–1971, and Marie-Francine Oppeneau, 1931–2023)

Poster House Permanent Collection

- In the immediate postwar period, the French Standardization Association (AFNOR) updated the quality and safety requirements needed to sell appliances within France. These new restrictions resulted in fewer options on the domestic market but encouraged mass production and cheaper prices.
- Rather than promoting specific brands, the posters produced by EDF typically highlighted the joys of a generic electrical appliance in order to encourage citizens to purchase such items for their homes and take advantage of affordable electricity.
- Here, a mermaid with a tail composed of an electrical cord hugs her new water heater. The tagline reads "cheap electric hot water." Uncomplicated, direct messages like these helped combat the misconception that electric appliances were luxury items not meant for the middle-class consumer. Despite this, until very recently, most electric boilers in France were powered by imported oil or methane.
- SODEL (the Society for the Development of Electricity Applications), whose name appears at the lower right, was a subsidiary of EDF that published many posters promoting electricity during the 1950s and 1960s.

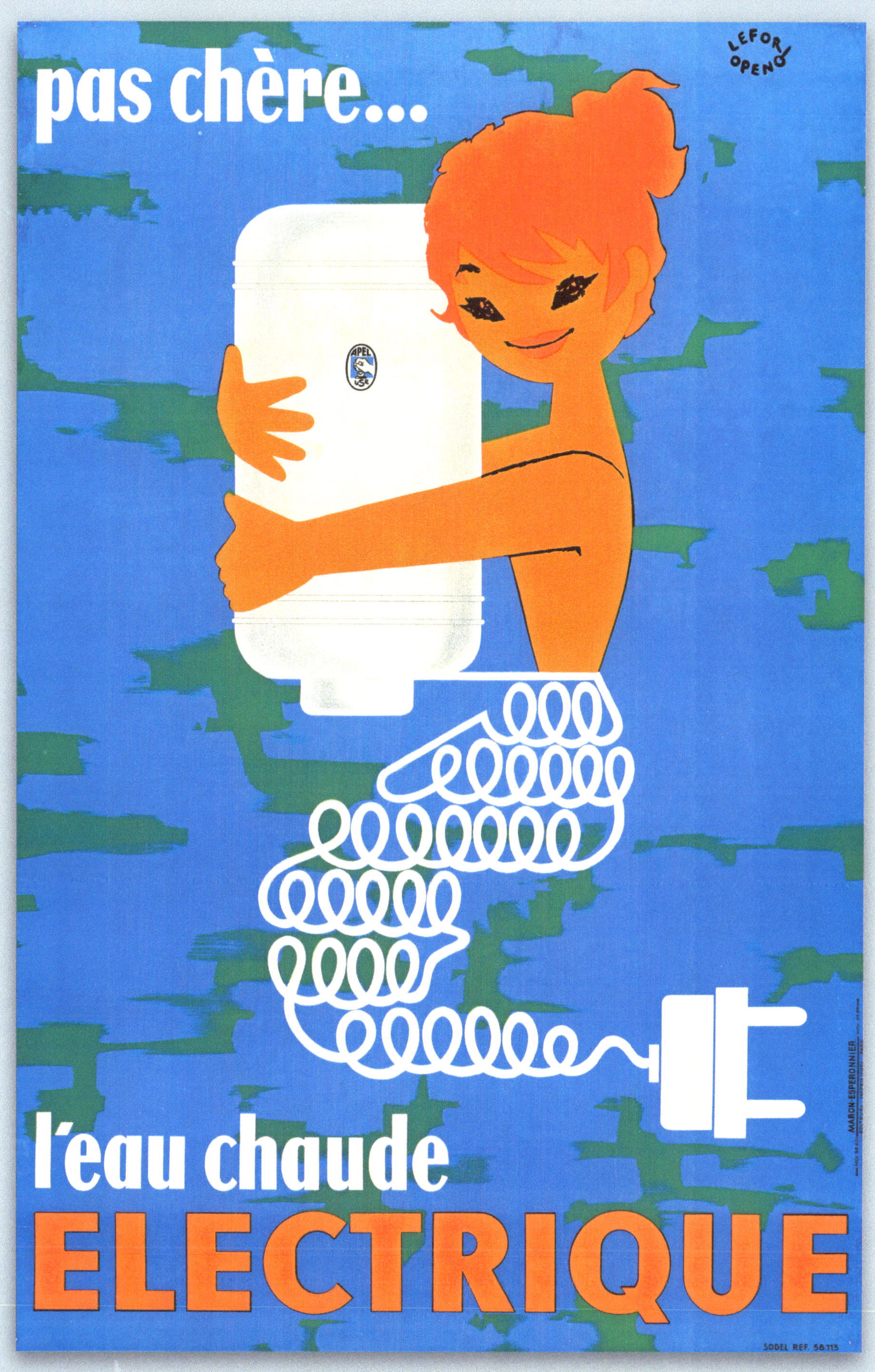
pas chère...
LEFOR
OPENO
APEL
l'eau chaude
ELECTRIQUE
MARON-ESPERONNIER
SODEL REF. 58.113

offrez des cadeaux

...

ÉLECTRIQUES

LEFOR OPENO

Edité par SODEL

Offrez des Cadeaux...Électriques, 1959

Lefor-Openo (Marie-Claire Lefort, 1931–1971, and Marie-Francine Oppeneau, 1931–2023)

Private Collection, NYC

- Rather than highlighting a specific appliance, this advertising postcard (also produced as a large poster) simply says "give electric gifts."
- While many of Lefor-Openo's designs feature an upbeat, modern portrayal of femininity, many of their advertising conceits reflect the masculinist reality of 1950s' and 1960s' France. Although women had been constitutionally granted equal salaries to men in 1946, official language and policies still encouraged them to stay home. Nearly every political group, from the Christian Democrats to the Socialists, the Communists to the unions, saw a woman's primary roles as those of wife and mother—and advertising of the time reinforced that omnipresent view.
- Here, the idea that the most romantic gift one can buy a woman is an appliance encourages male viewers to equate their suitability as a mate with their ability to purchase modern housewares for their wives, reaffirming traditional gender roles.

J'ai Une Machine à Laver, 1959

Lefor-Openo (Marie-Claire Lefort, 1931–1971, and Marie-Francine Oppeneau, 1931–2023)

Poster House Permanent Collection

- Between 1950 and 1958, appliance production in France increased by more than 400 percent. While far less prevalent in modern homes than electric stoves, water heaters, and refrigerators, domestic washing machines were promoted as essential additions to contemporary life.
- "White goods" (an industry term for appliances) were almost exclusively advertised in terms of their benefits to women, turning chores into what appeared to be effortless, even glamorous, work. While traditional female labor was not actually changing, the ways in which it was depicted in advertising were: women were now the heroes of the household—sexualized, satisfied, and empowered by technology.
- Here, Lefor-Openo presents a buxom redhead carrying a pile of perfectly folded sheets and towels on her head as she announces that she has a washing machine. The implication is that the type of modern woman who owns such a device has the time to maintain her girlish sensuality while simultaneously managing an idealized domestic life for her family. Advertisers of the time believed that this type of promotion was "liberating" to women, not objectifying.

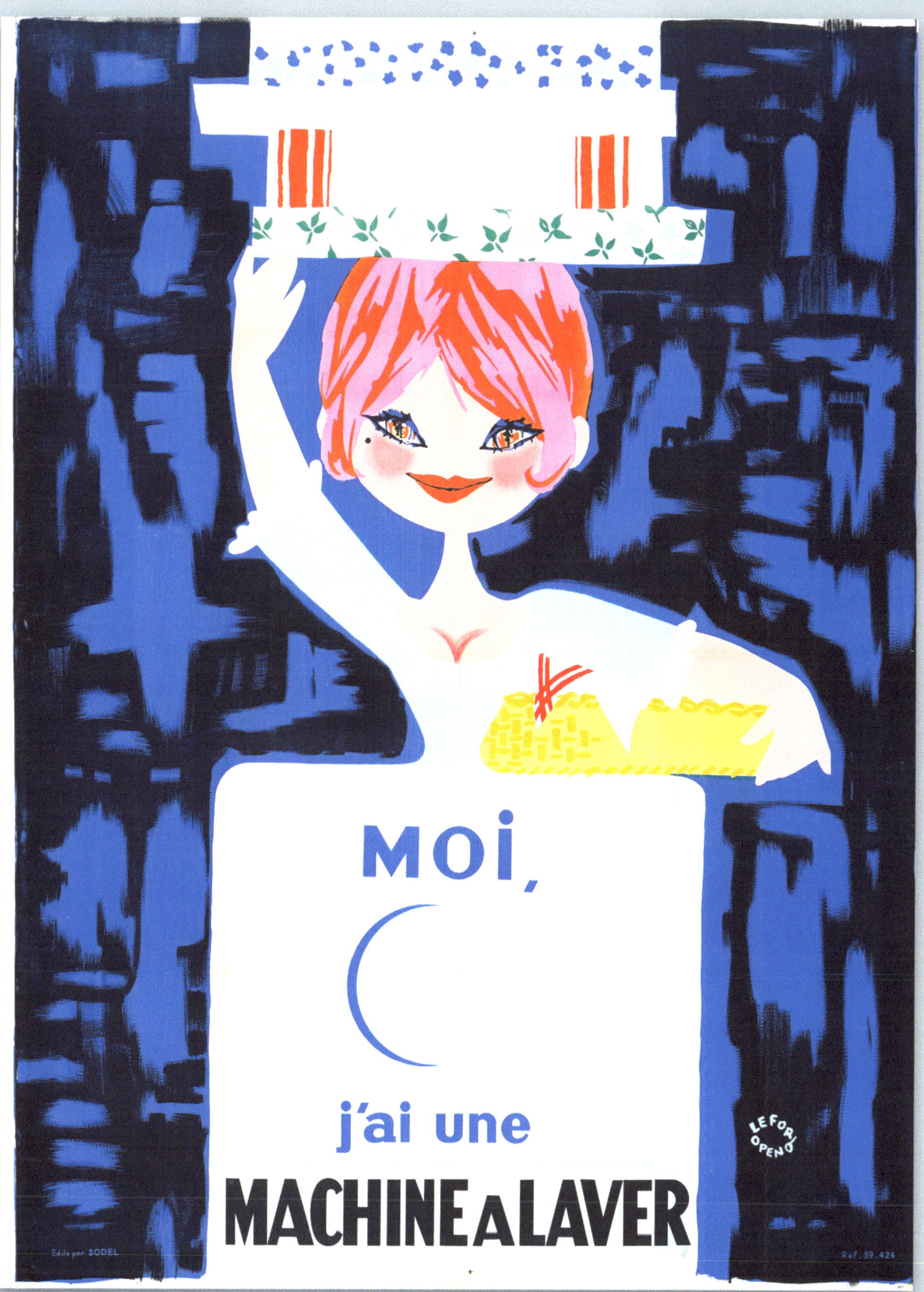
MOI,
C
j'ai une
MACHINE A LAVER
LEFOR OPENO
Edité par SODEL
Réf. 59.424

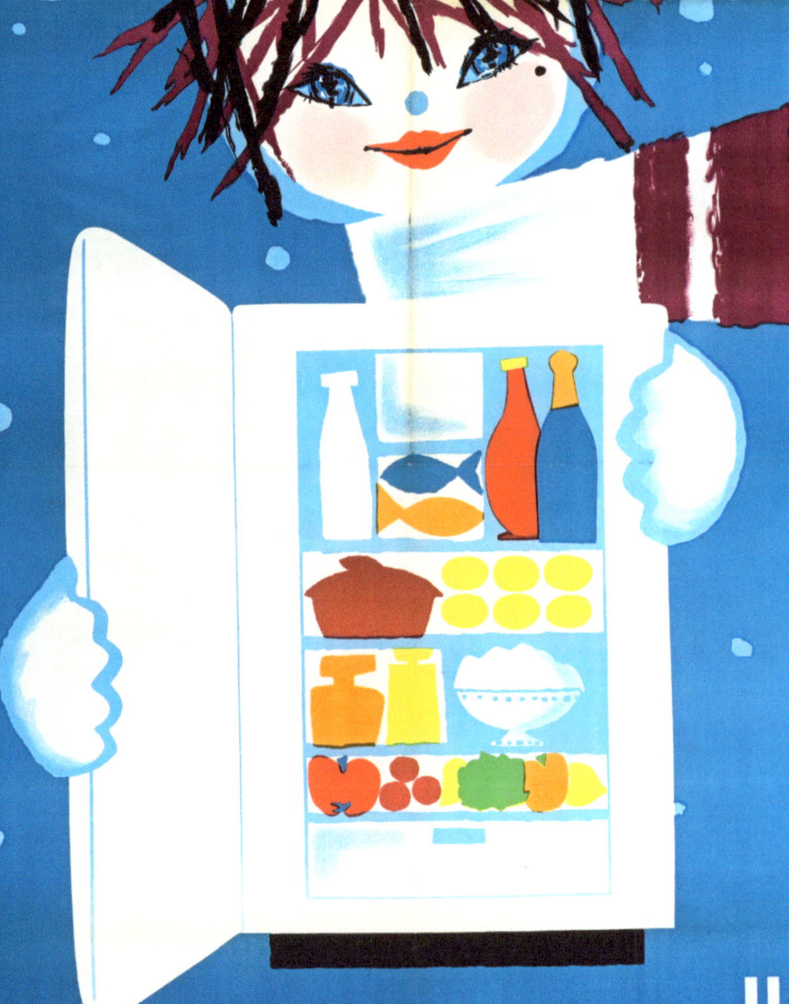
hiver comme été ...
LEFOR OPENO
... un
RÉFRIGÉRATEUR
Edité par SODEL
Réf. 59-319

Réfrigérateur, 1959

Lefor-Openo (Marie-Claire Lefort, 1931–1971, and Marie-Francine Oppeneau, 1931–2023)

Poster House Permanent Collection

- When many women were forced to enter the workforce during World War I, they could no longer dedicate as much time to domestic labor, including the purchasing and preparing of food. Refrigerators were introduced during the interwar period as a solution to this problem; they kept perishables fresher for longer and thus reduced the number of trips to the market.
- Early domestic refrigerators were prohibitively expensive (both to purchase and to power) and were associated with the upper classes, often advertised with images showing a maid using them or filled with extravagant items like champagne. This dramatically changed, however, with the advent of EDF and the standardization of appliances. In 1954, only around 6.7 percent of all French households had refrigerators. By 1962, that number had risen to 40.3 percent; by 1970, it was 90 percent.
- The increase in advertising for domestic appliances meant that many artists used similar motifs, taglines, and conceits when promoting the same products. Hervé Morvan, a more prominent and prolific male designer of the period, incorporates an inversion of the same caption used in Lefor-Openo's poster, showing instead a giraffe turning into a penguin inside a Brandt refrigerator.

Électricité de France, 1960

Lefor-Openo (Marie-Claire Lefort, 1931–1971, and Marie-Francine Oppeneau, 1931–2023)
Poster House Permanent Collection

- de Gaulle's ambitious plans for energy self-sufficiency required funding. Almost every year from the mid-1950s to 1975, the government launched a bond that allowed the public to invest in the energy sector, providing capital for the construction of numerous key projects, including coal-fueled and hydroelectric power stations as well as general improvements to the national grid.
- Participation in these types of government-issued bond programs was not just seen as a reliable financial investment, but also as an expression of French solidarity and faith in the current administration.
- Rather than relying on their smiling signature character to promote this endeavor, Lefor-Openo turned a cleverly bent electrical cord and two bipin lightbulbs into a Gallic rooster, the national symbol of France.
- The impact of de Gaulle's vision for energy self-sufficiency still resonates today: thanks to the infrastructure created through this and other bond programs, France generates approximately 95 percent of its electricity from low-carbon domestic sources.

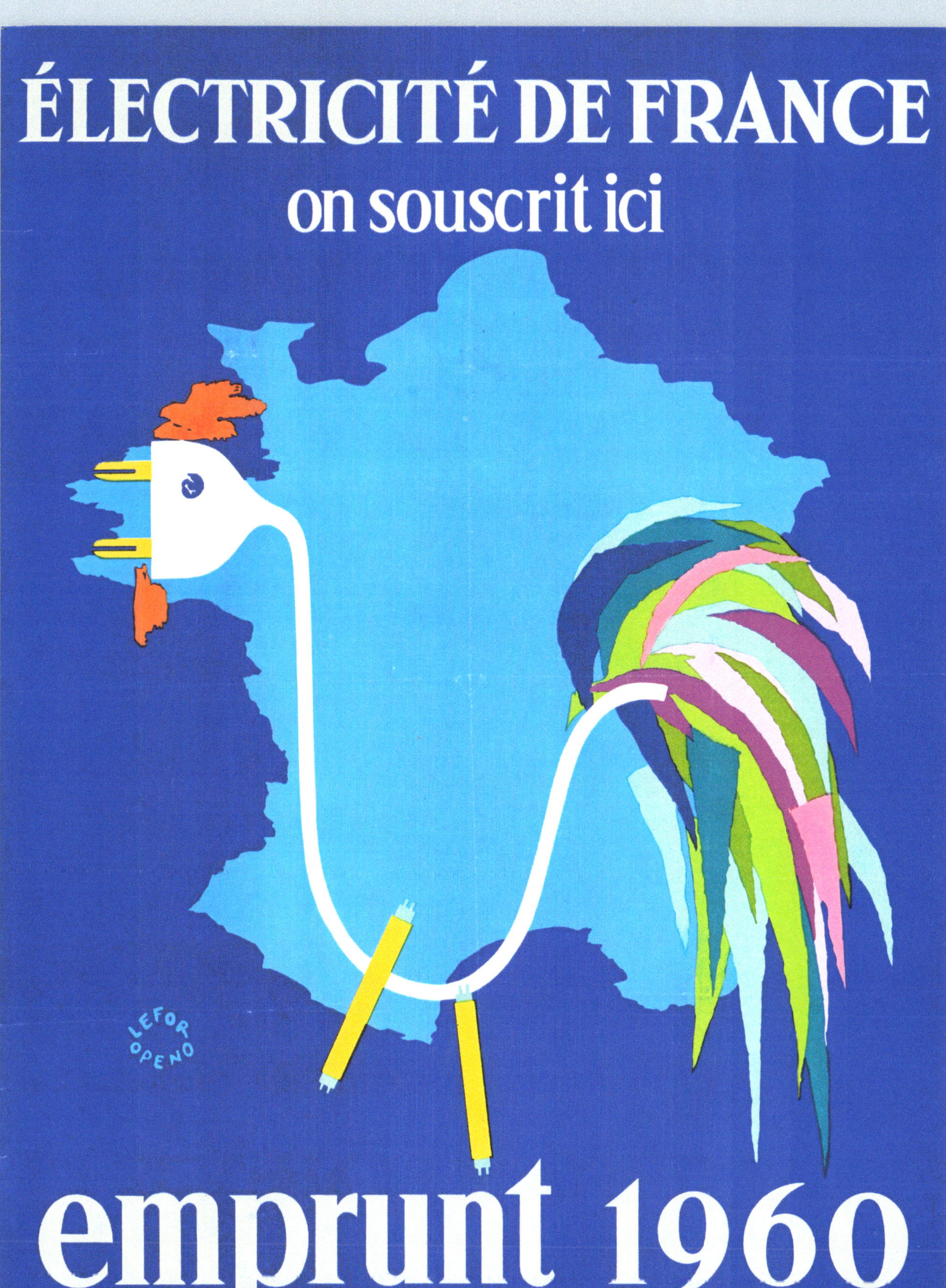
ÉLECTRICITÉ DE FRANCE
on souscrit ici
LEFOR OPENO
emprunt 1960
EDITÉ PAR SODEL
55, Rue de Naples, PARIS

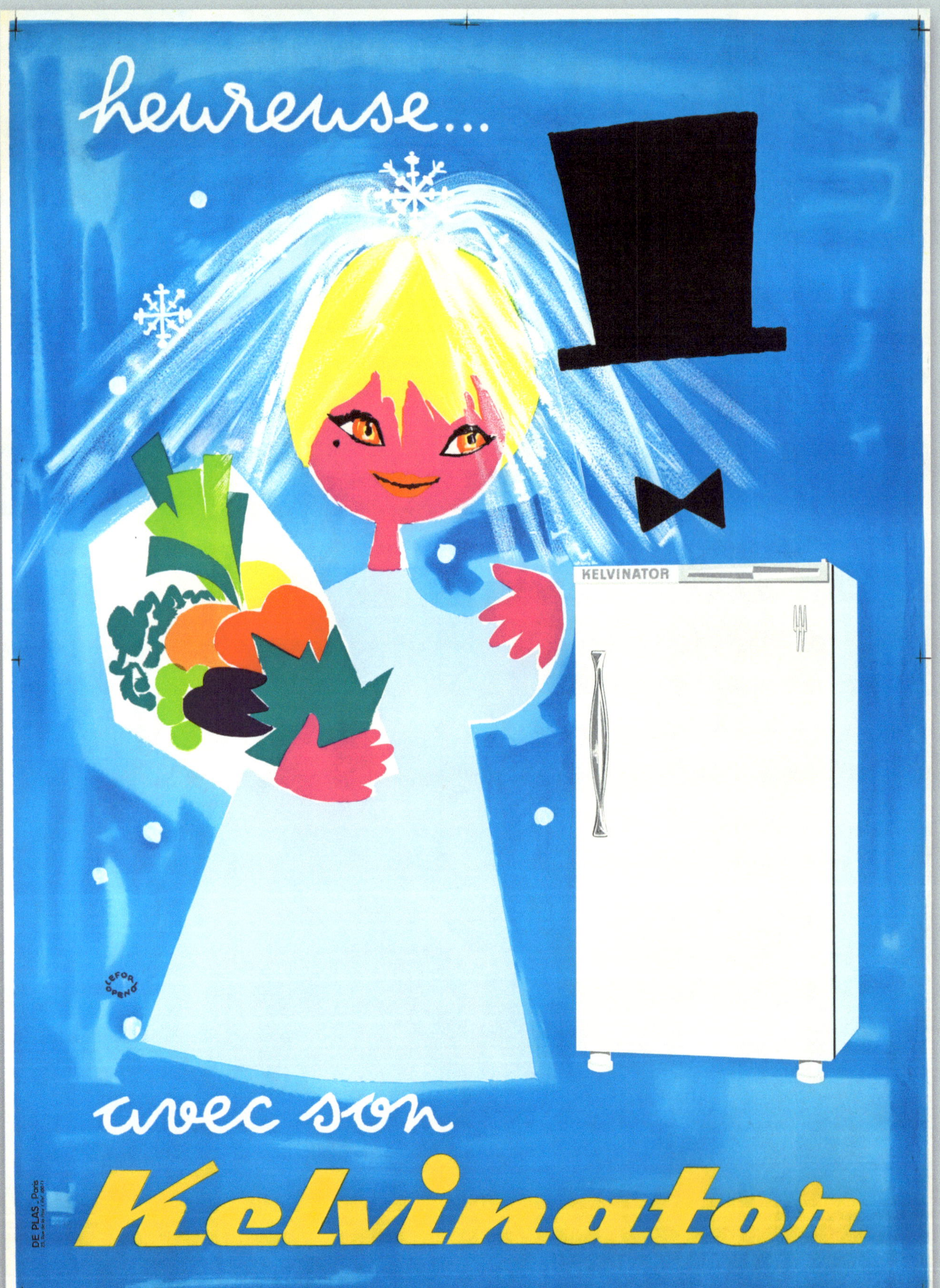
heureuse...
KELVINATOR
LEFOR OPENO
avec son
Kelvinator
DE PLAS - Paris

Kelvinator, 1961

Lefor-Openo (Marie-Claire Lefort, 1931–1971, and Marie-Francine Oppeneau, 1931–2023)

Poster House Permanent Collection

- EDF's electricity campaign proved so effective that private companies began using many of the same artists and advertising strategies to promote their own products. Here, Lefor-Openo uses their signature character to show a "happy" young bride married to her Kelvinator refrigerator (a name derived from the Kelvin temperature scale, in which the lowest-possible temperature is "absolute zero").
- Many companies incorporated marriage-coded iconography in their advertisements to suggest that a certain item was essential for any couple starting a new life together. These strategies set the standard for how the modern French home was expected to look and function.
- Starting in 1938, France introduced a generous system of benefits and incentives for people to get married and have children. At the time this poster was issued, tax relief and financial subsidies were given to those who had multiple offspring, and loans were offered to young rural couples to fund their new homes. Further benefits were available to people who had children within two years of marriage, discouraging women from entering the workforce in order to receive such assistance.

Eau Chaude, 1962

Lefor-Openo (Marie-Claire Lefort, 1931–1971, and Marie-Francine Oppeneau, 1931–2023)

Poster House Permanent Collection

- This is one of at least three variants of this design extolling an electric water heater as a "trump card for your individual comfort." This turn of phrase is further reflected in the general composition of the poster, which resembles a playing card.
- Despite marketing efforts to indicate otherwise, many consumers were worried that their old electricity meters could not handle the increased demand put on them by so many new appliances. In 1963, EDF introduced the Blue Meter, promoting it as the most efficient way to update the home for modern electric use. Many posters from this period, including those by Lefor-Openo, use the same blue hue as the meter to link them in the consumer's mind.
- The new meter was actually the same as the old meter, just painted a different color. The real modifications that allowed for increased electric usage were applied to the network; however, the public felt more secure believing that the updates were occurring in their own homes.

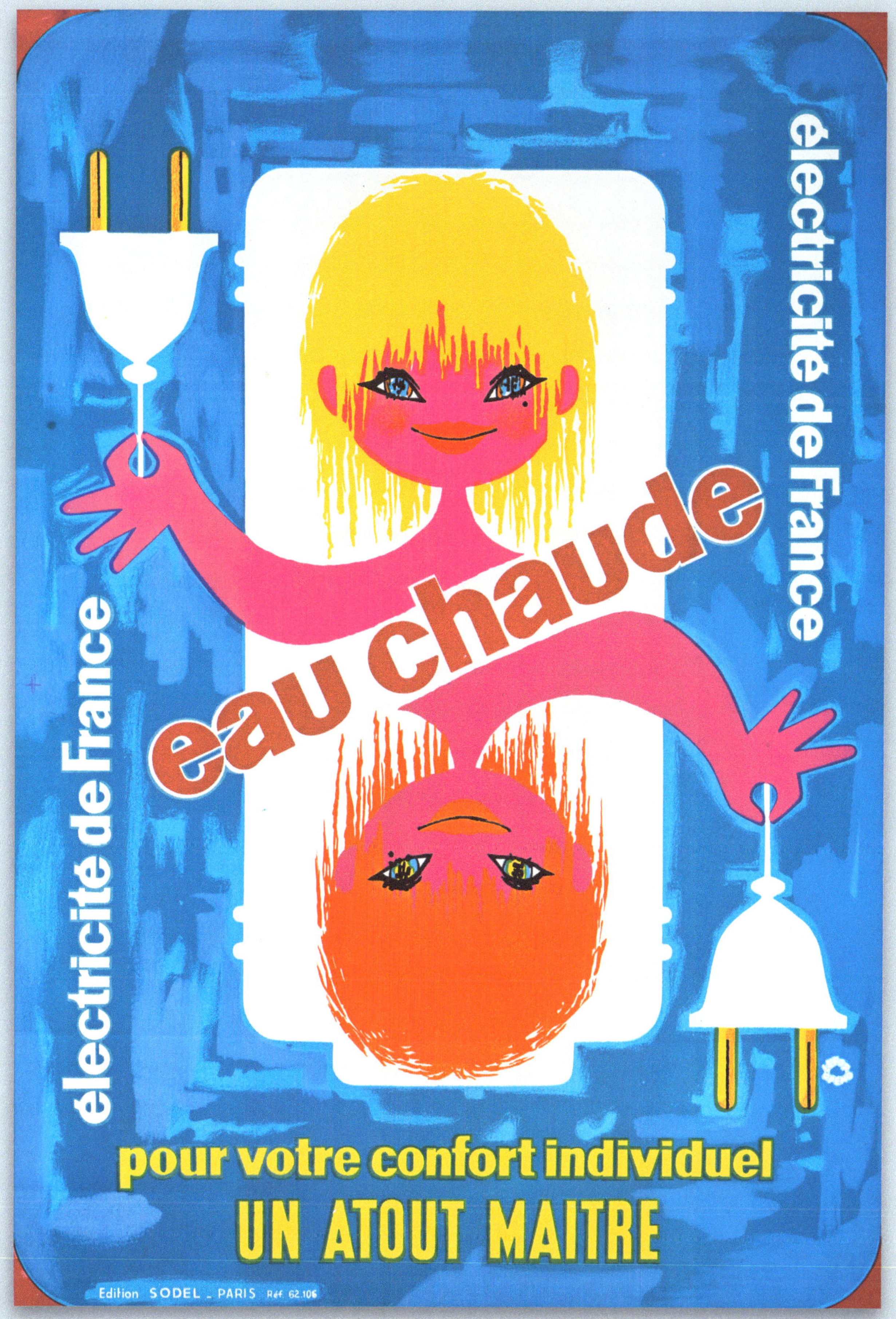
électricité de France
électricité de France
eau chaude
pour votre confort individuel
UN ATOUT MAITRE
Edition SODEL _ PARIS Réf. 62.106

EDF

vous présente

Anne-Marie
CARRIERE
et
Pierre-Jean
VAILLARD

pour votre
confort

LE CHAUFFE-EAU
ÉLECTRIQUE

HAVAS CONSEIL

Anne-Marie Carriere et Pierre-Jean Vaillard, c. 1960

Lefor-Openo (Marie-Claire Lefort, 1931–1971,
and Marie-Francine Oppeneau, 1931–2023)
Private Collection, NYC

- Flexi-discs are a type of paper-thin plastic record that gained commercial popularity in the 1960s. Typically offered as a free gift with purchase, they were usually spoken endorsements or infomercials for a product, often voiced by minor celebrities. Because of their flimsy construction, they could only be played a few times before the grooves were worn down, making the record unusable.
- This flexi-disc was created by EDF with a cover illustration by Lefor-Openo to promote the purchase of electric water heaters. It features the vocal talents of Anne-Marie Carrière and Pierre-Jean Vaillard, both of whom had long careers as character actors.
- Until the 1950s, bathtubs were the primary method of bathing in homes; however, heating a bath takes an extraordinary amount of water and energy. Even with the widespread adoption of improved electric water heaters, most could not provide enough warm water to facilitate a bath. Because of this, indoor showers became increasingly popular throughout the 1950s and '60s and became the main method of bathing in the '70s.

La Vie Heureuse par l'Électricité, 1963

Lefor-Openo (Marie-Claire Lefort, 1931–1971, and Marie-Francine Oppeneau, 1931–2023)
Private Collection, NYC

- Designed to absorb excess wet ink from fountain pens, blotting paper was a common desk accessory in the early 20th century and was frequently offered as a giveaway item by companies; these sheets featured small advertisements that would live on the recipient's desk for a few weeks. While the use of blotting paper declined in the 1950s with the advent of the ballpoint pen, it was not entirely retired until the 1970s. A decorative blotter like this would have been sent in the mail by EDF or given away at an appliance store to promote the purchase of a variety of electric goods.
- Here, Lefor-Openo provides a vision of a "happy life" thanks to a fully electrified kitchen that incorporates a water heater, a stove, a washing machine, and a refrigerator. Such an abundance of new technology would have been difficult for most French families to afford in the early 1960s. These fantasies of the ideal home were based on an American standard, so much so that many television commercials for modern appliances were shot in suburban kitchens in the United States rather than in France.

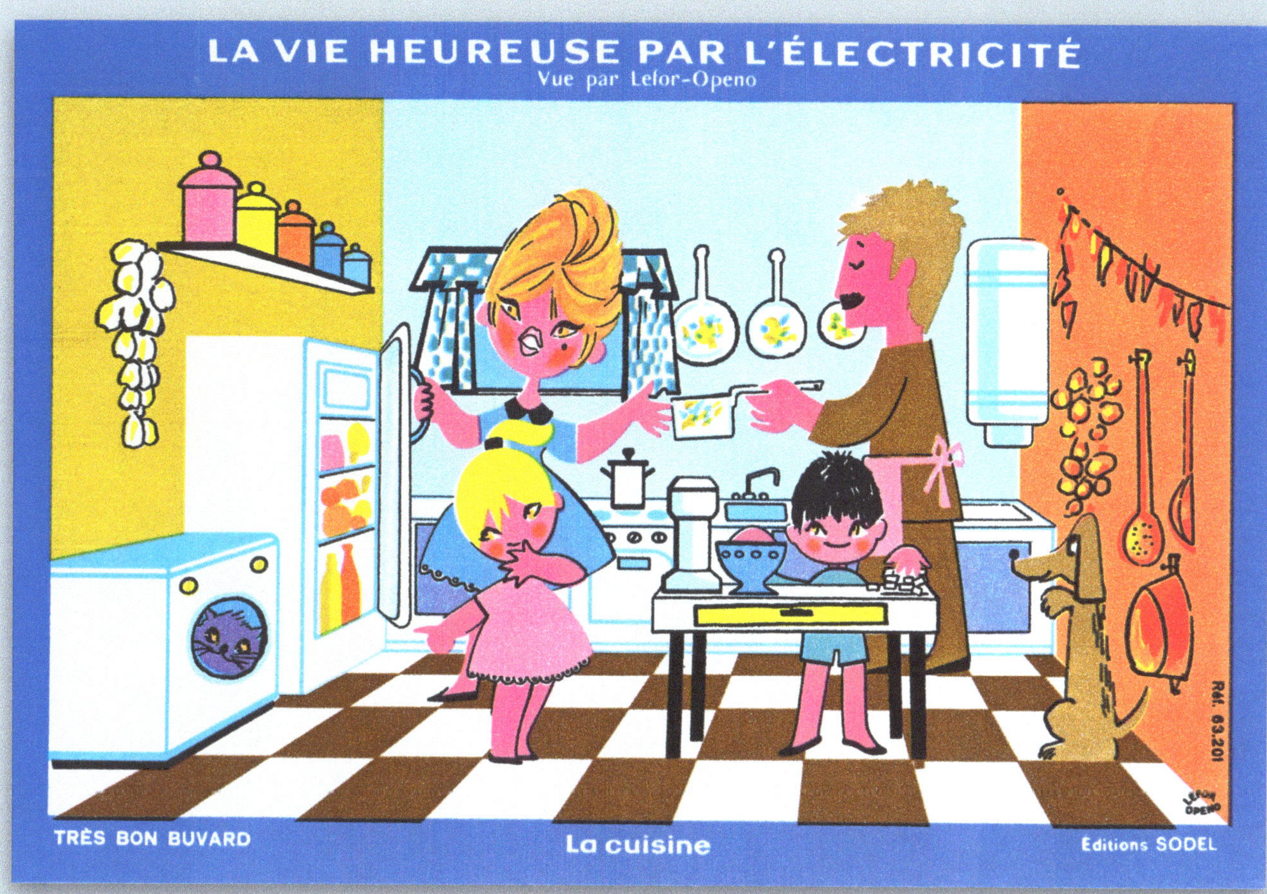
LA VIE HEUREUSE PAR L'ÉLECTRICITÉ
Vue par Lefor-Openo
Réf. 63.201
LEFOR OPENO
TRÈS BON BUVARD
La cuisine
Editions SODEL

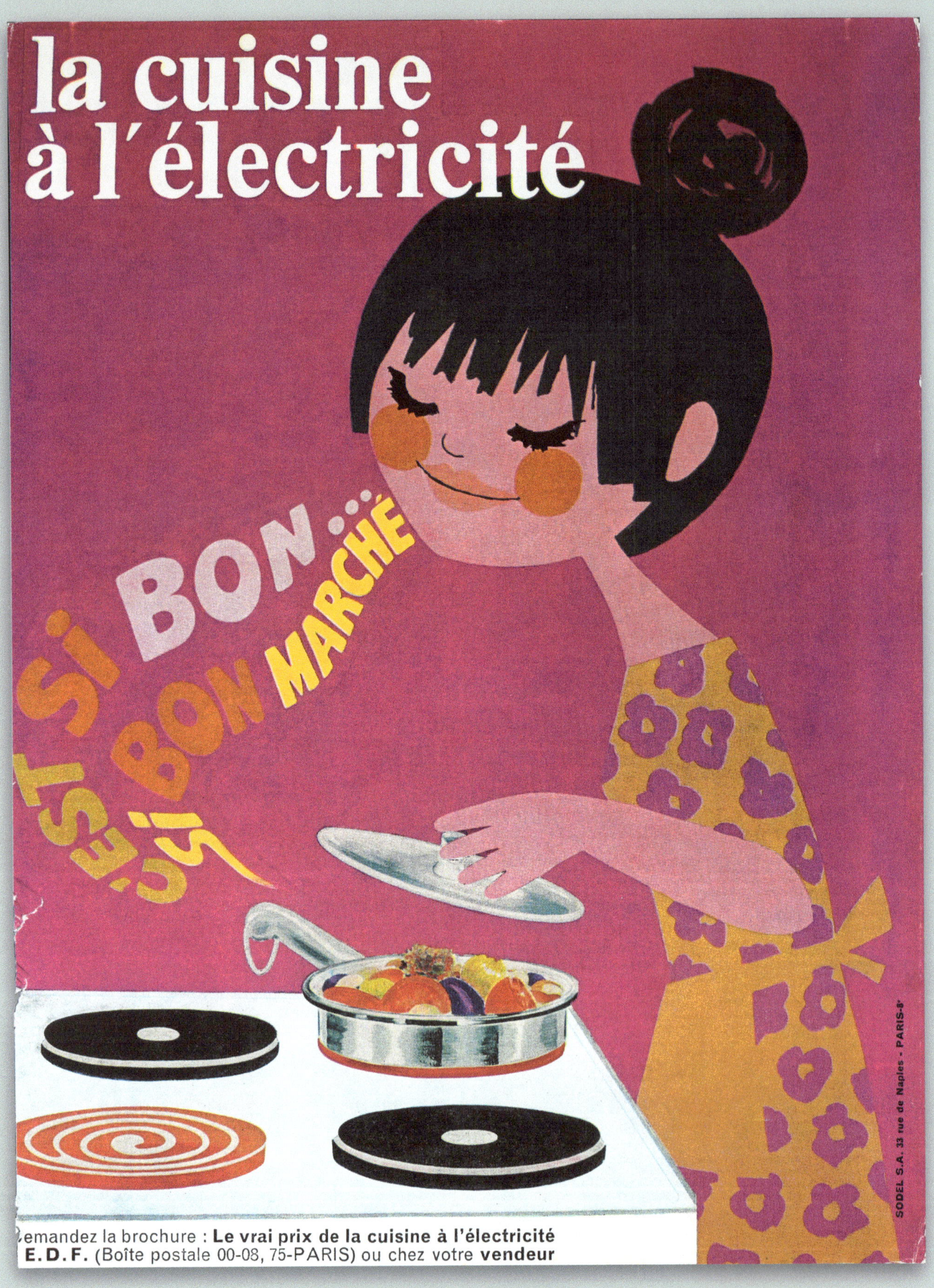

la cuisine
à l'électricité
C'EST SI BON...
C'EST SI BON MARCHÉ
emandez la brochure : **Le vrai prix de la cuisine à l'électricité**
E.D.F. (Boîte postale 00-08, 75-PARIS) ou chez votre **vendeur**
SODEL S.A. 33 rue de Naples - PARIS-8e

La Cuisine à l'Électricité, c. 1965

Lefor-Openo (Marie-Claire Lefort, 1931–1971, and Marie-Francine Oppeneau, 1931–2023)
Private Collection, NYC

- Lefor-Openo worked with EDF from 1958 to 1967. This magazine advertisement is most likely one of their last designs for the company, as indicated by the updated fashion of their signature female figure. The image proved so popular that EDF rereleased it in 1979 as nuclear power gradually took over; it ran with the tagline "electricity is clean and so modern." Here, however, it simply states that the electric kitchen is "so good, so cheap," with instructions at the bottom to request a brochure from either EDF or a local appliance dealer to find out more about how affordable an upgraded kitchen can be.
- The electric stove was a massive improvement on the coal-powered ovens that had preceded them because they enabled much more variation in and control over the amount of heat. With electricity, women no longer needed to strictly monitor a meal and could adjust the intensity of the heat quickly and easily.
- While not visible in this composition, electric stoves also allowed for the introduction of glass oven doors through which a chef could more easily watch the food as it cooked. Innovations like these were often linked in advertising with ideas of modernity and technology that young consumers found exciting.

Le Numéro de la Lumière, c. 1965
Lefor-Openo (Marie-Claire Lefort, 1931–1971, and Marie-Francine Oppeneau, 1931–2023)
Private Collection, NYC

- The government's efforts to promote energy consumption were extremely successful. In the period between 1963 and 1964 alone, more than half of those who updated their electric meters also purchased at least one large electrical appliance. The fully electrified home was now a staple of everyday French life.
- In this magazine advertisement, a young woman with a trendy bouffant hairstyle is taking advantage of the free "lighting hotline" provided by the Paris Electricity Center to discuss decor options for her home. This marks a shift in consumer relations, indicating that suppliers were no longer just providing a utility but also offering their support and advice on how electricity could best be used by and tailored to the individual—not simply as an amenity but as a stamp of creative expression.

LE CENTRE DE PARIS - ÉLECTRICITÉ

vous propose gratuitement

SES CONSEILS SUR L'ÉCLAIRAGE

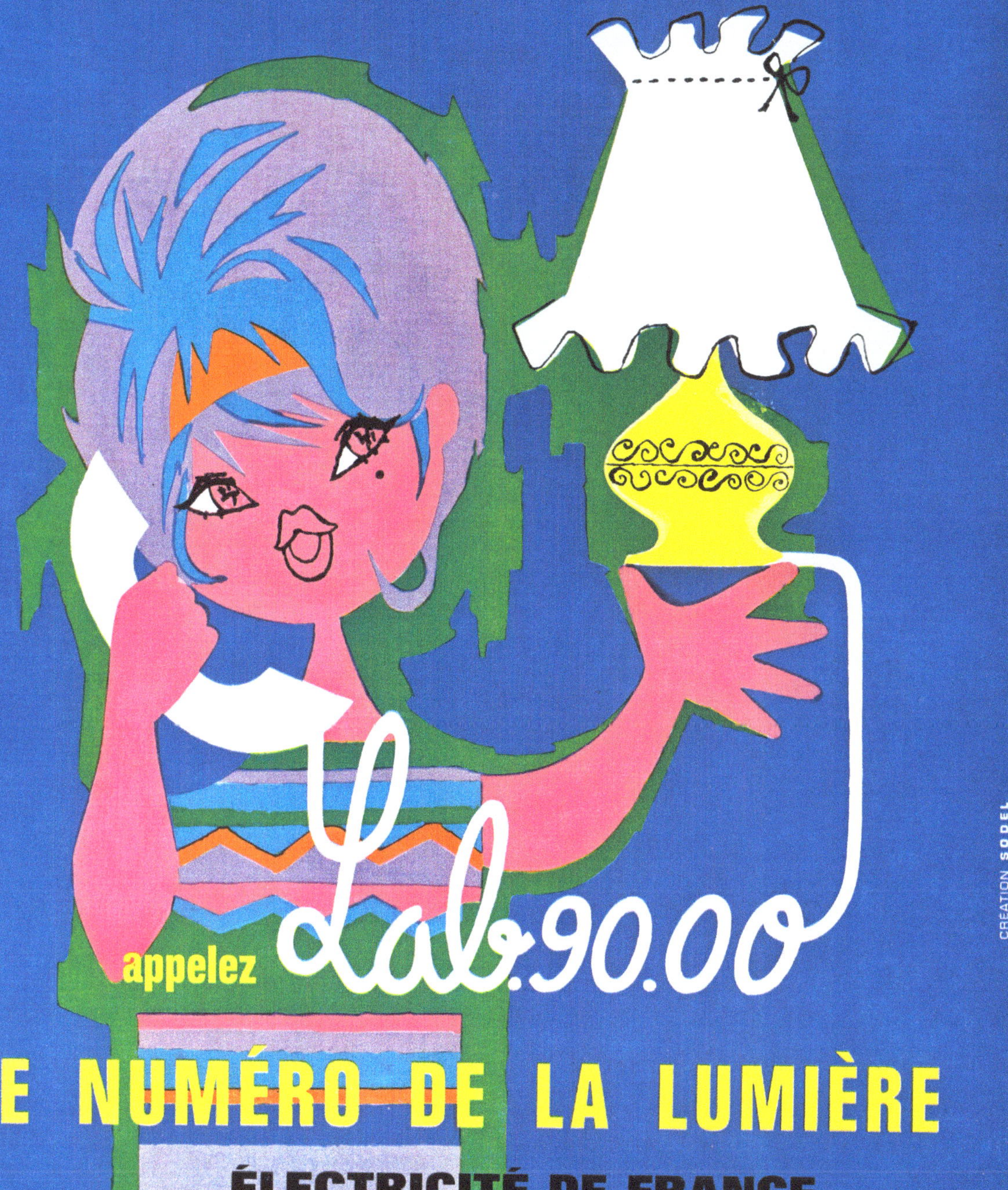

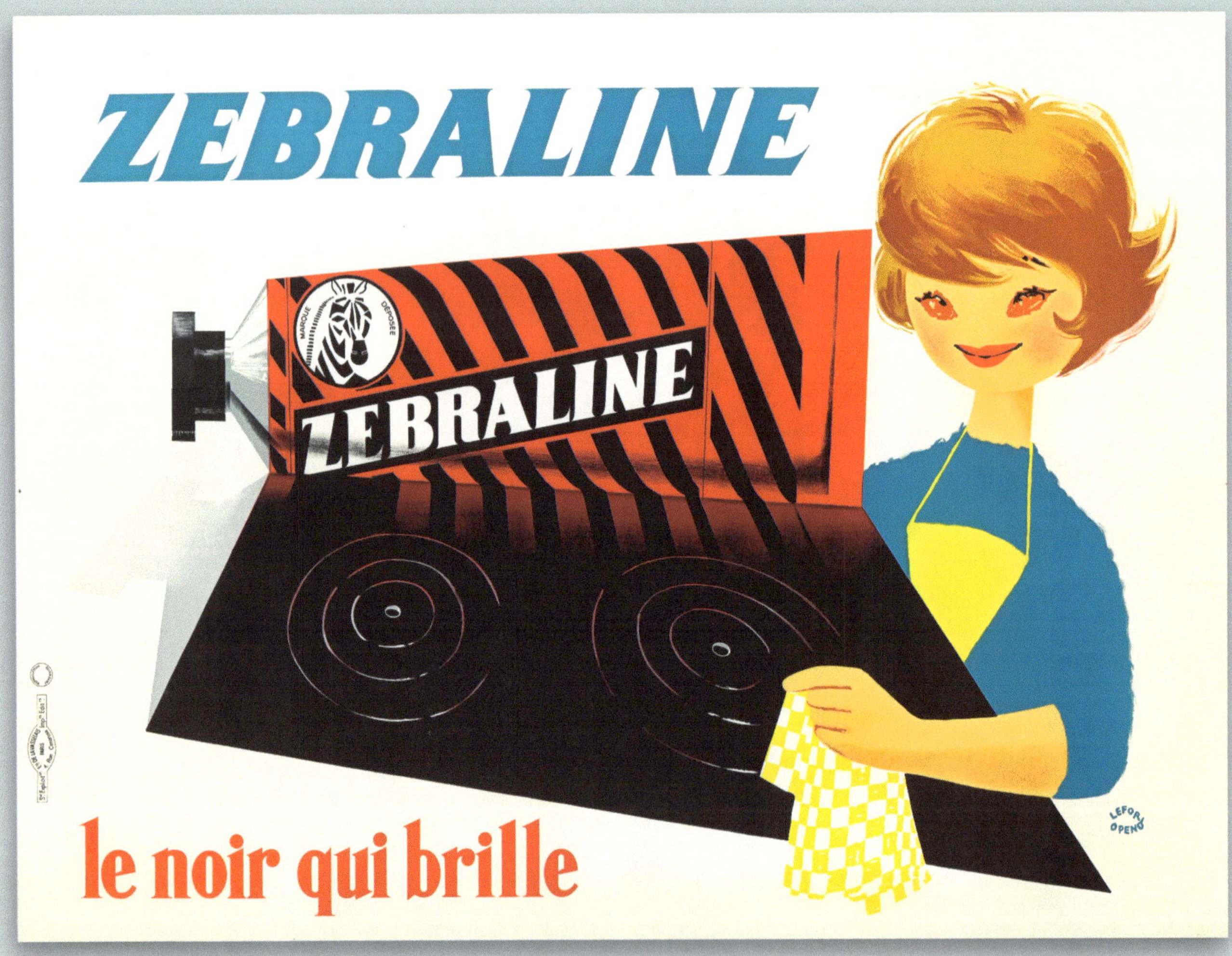
ZEBRALINE
MARQUE DÉPOSÉE
ZEBRALINE
le noir qui brille
LEFOR OPENO

Zebraline, 1959

Lefor-Openo (Marie-Claire Lefort, 1931–1971, and Marie-Francine Oppeneau, 1931–2023)

Poster House Permanent Collection

- Like Kelvinator, Zebraline was so charmed by Lefor-Openo's work for EDF that it wanted to incorporate their signature female figure into its advertising. In this way, the two designers became victims of their own success, continually asked to replicate a formula for everything from sewing machines to—in this case—stove polish.
- While still very much within the visual language of their typical character, this poster presents a more mature woman polishing an electric stove. Such slight variations in their figure's appearance as she performs similar domestic tasks suggests that traditional gender roles were reinforced across generations—the modern French woman, whether 18 or 48, was, first and foremost, a housewife.

André Huet, c. 1960

Lefor-Openo (Marie-Claire Lefort, 1931–1971, and Marie-Francine Oppeneau, 1931–2023)

Poster House Permanent Collection

- André Huet was a French textile manufacturer specializing in bedding, napkins, and other domestic goods up through the late 1960s, when it was absorbed into a larger company. Its advertisements all included 3+3+3 as an indication of the high thread count (300 strands per square centimeter) of its products, lending them softness and durability that could, as stated in this poster, last three generations.
- In French advertising of the 1950s and '60s, images of the modern, youthful woman were often combined with scenes of good housekeeping, incorporating two modes of thought that were being challenged in much of the Western world.
- Appliances were not the only housewares subject to innovation at this time: in 1959, the fitted bottom sheet was patented, allowing mattresses to stay cleaner and women to make beds faster.
- This design by Lefor-Openo was also issued in a smaller format with a bright-red background and the outline of a house around the three women, showing how a company might adopt a given composition for various advertising outlets.

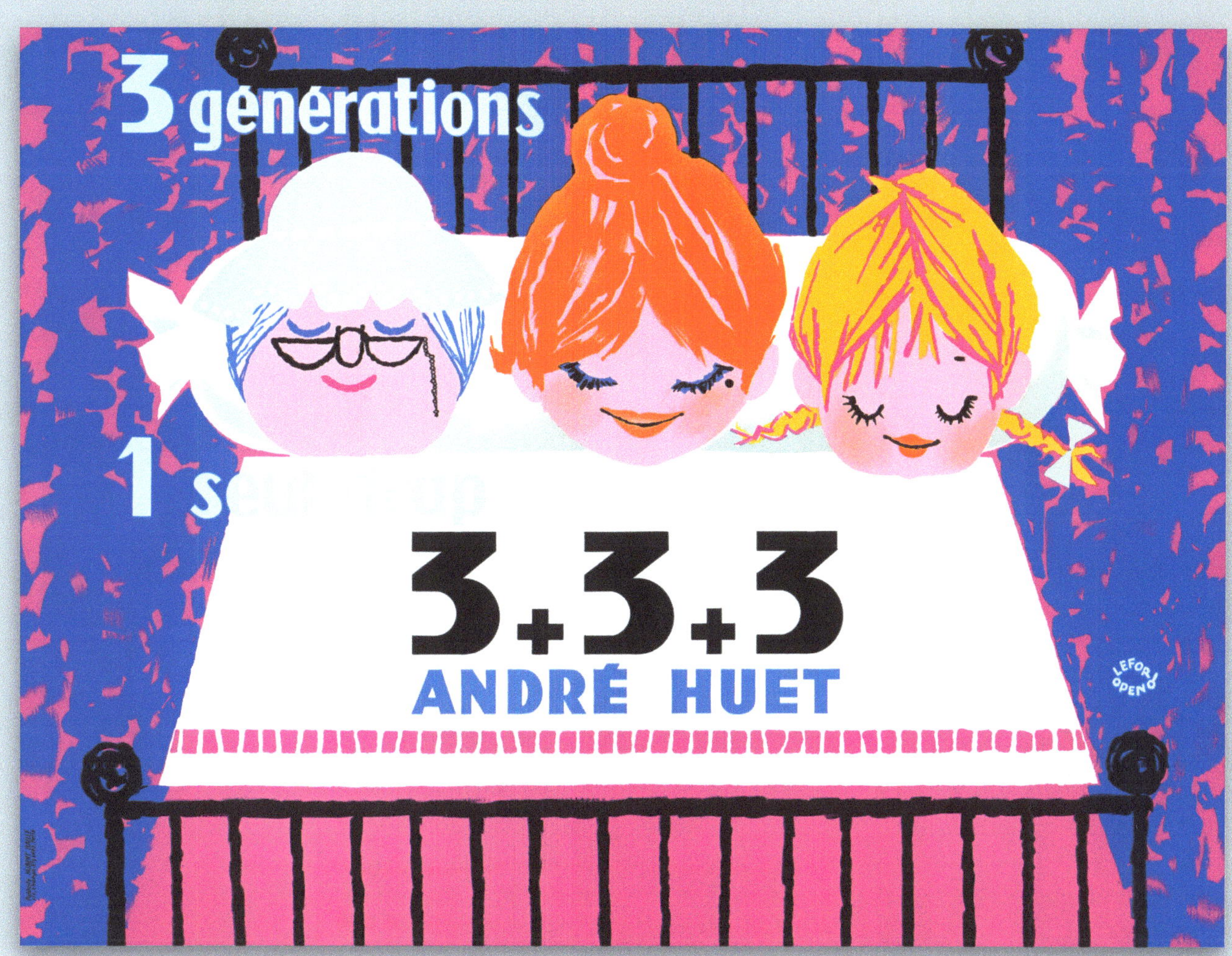
3 générations
3+3+3
ANDRÉ HUET
LEFOR OPENO

MIDDLE-CLASS CONSUMERISM

Beyond politics and a state-dominated economy, Charles de Gaulle's France was deeply shaped by the influence of the growing middle class. While not a monolith, most people within this group shared views on what modern French society should be and how its citizens should behave. The middle classes valued stability and tradition, particularly when it came to the role of women and the larger family unit. Although they maintained a strong sense of bourgeois frugality, they also enjoyed the expanded purchasing power allowed by the growing economy and indulged in products, entertainment, and leisure pursuits that previous generations would not have thought possible. While not all of Lefor-Openo's posters for individual companies or events were of national importance, they all reflected this middle-class sensibility over what modern France represented to itself.

Vichy, c. 1958

Lefor-Openo (Marie-Claire Lefort, 1931–1971, and Marie-Francine Oppeneau, 1931–2023)

Poster House Permanent Collection

- One of Lefor-Openo's best-known advertising images, this poster fully embraces Mayor Pierre Coulon's vision for a new Vichy. Issued as a general travel campaign both domestically and throughout Europe, it promotes the many leisure activities, from sports to gambling, that can be enjoyed in the region.
- While some poster historians have claimed that the central figure is meant to be the actress Brigitte Bardot, who wore a similar dress for her marriage to Jacques Charrier in 1959, there is no evidence that this is the case (not least because the poster was printed before their wedding). The distinctive pink gingham is more likely a reference to Vichy check, a fabric historically associated with the region.
- Some historians have also asked if the same figure is intended to be a Black woman. While impossible to state with certainty, Lefor-Openo created a handful of posters featuring elegant, sophisticated Black women as well as designs that incorporated racist stereotypes. Since Vichy was a wealthy spa town eager to attract an upper-class clientele, it is more likely that the figure has a deep suntan—a trend among the jet-setters who wanted to show off their ability to travel to sunny locations all year round.
- This composition was so well received that it was reprinted and reused internationally in 1960.

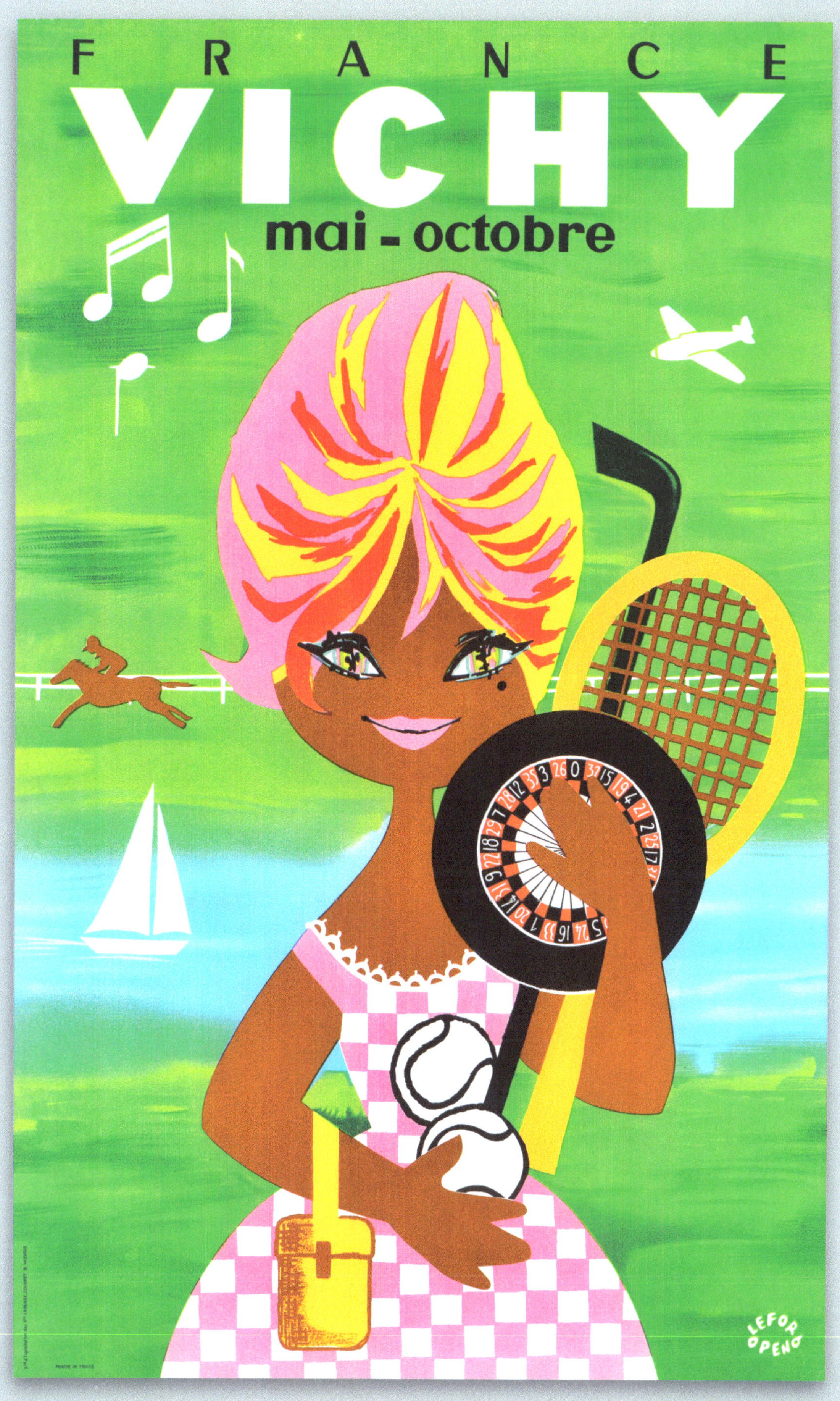
FRANCE
VICHY
mai - octobre
LEFOR OPENO

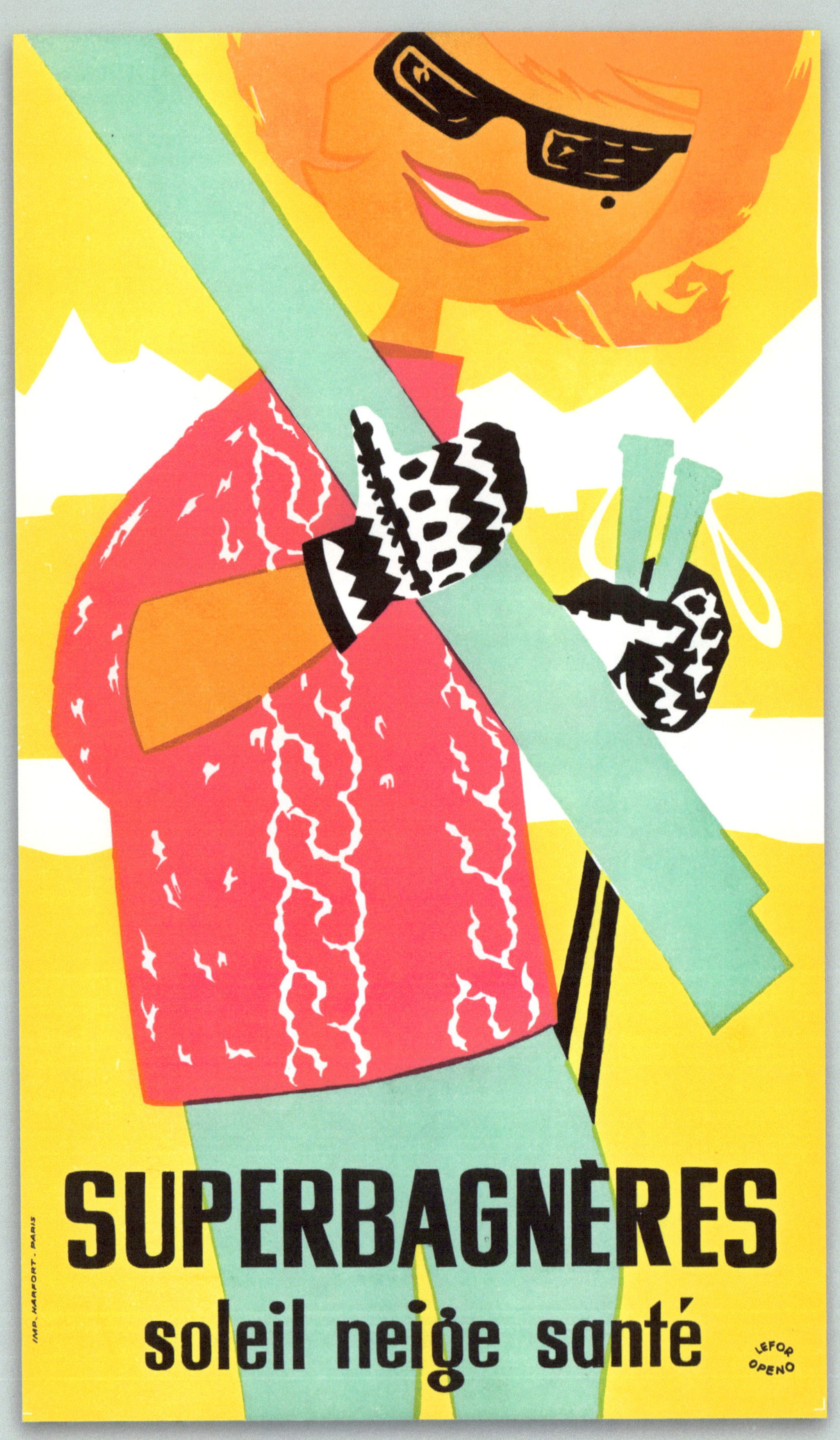
SUPERBAGNÈRES
soleil neige santé
IMP. HARFORT - PARIS
LEFOR
OPENO

Superbagnères, c. 1960

Lefor-Openo (Marie-Claire Lefort, 1931–1971, and Marie-Francine Oppeneau, 1931–2023)

Poster House Permanent Collection

- Lefor-Openo's travel poster for Vichy proved so successful in increasing tourism in the region that the Superbagnères ski resort in the Pyrenees mountains commissioned its own.
- After World War II, Superbagnères, like many spa towns and ski resorts in France, was forced to reconsider the nature of its clientele. It was no longer a playground for the ultrawealthy and needed to attract more middle-class visitors to remain profitable. Here, Lefor-Openo shows a modern, sporty woman in casual attire as the face of "sun, snow, and health" in the mountains.
- Many French companies encouraged domestic tourism after the war by offering travel vouchers and other benefits to their employees, thereby stimulating the local economy. Such efforts, along with the government's investment in infrastructure, contributed to the increasing ease and appeal of French travel.

Inter-Europe, c. 1960

Lefor-Openo (Marie-Claire Lefort, 1931–1971, and Marie-Francine Oppeneau, 1931–2023)
Poster House Permanent Collection

- Postwar prosperity meant that the middle classes now had disposable income that could be used to purchase everything from modern appliances to leisure travel. Agencies sprung up in major cities to cater to the many French citizens who now wanted to see the world. Owned by a female Polish emigrée, Inter-Europe in Paris was one such organization.
- Rather than paying Lefor-Openo to create an entire poster for Inter-Europe's roster of travel options, the company bought one of the pair's many illustrations and then inserted it into a simplified, geometric layout.
- As implied by the ski-to-sea themed couple, the destinations listed on the right are all-season resorts throughout Europe. While most of them are especially well known, Zakopane in Poland is a curious outlier and was most likely a point-of-pride addition by the owner of the travel agency.

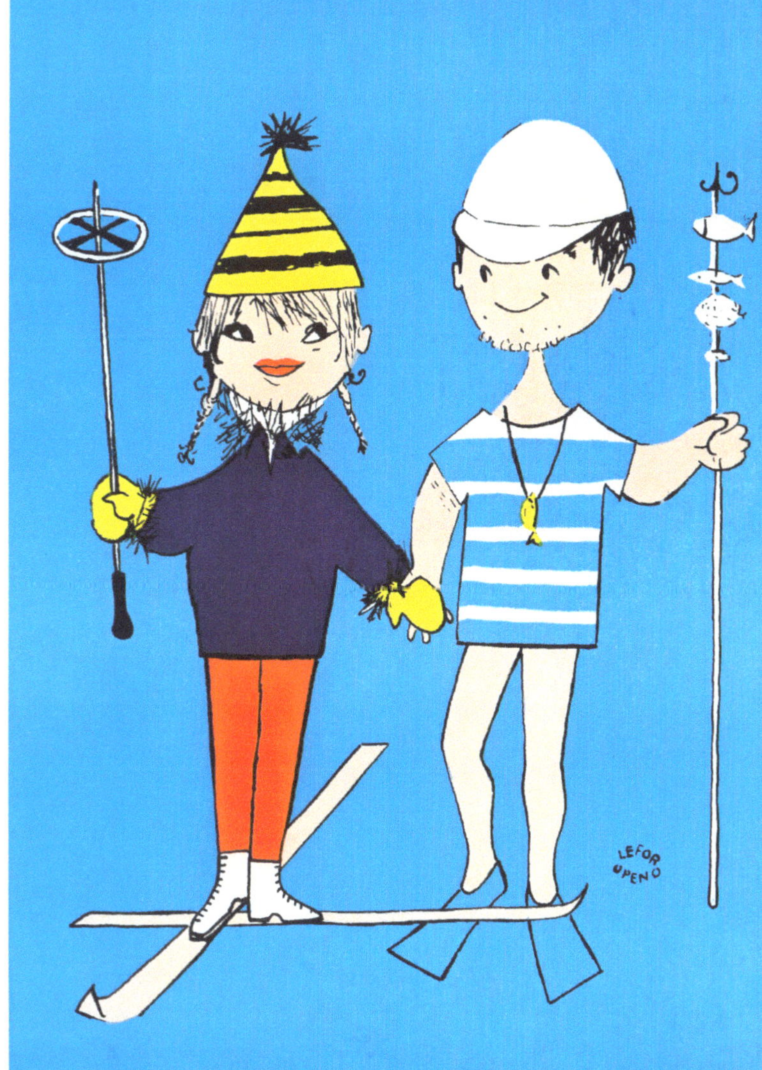
Ils partent ..... avec
inter - europe
Association du Tourisme pour Jeunes, Scolaires et Universitaires (Loi du 1er Juillet 1901)
22, Rue Gay-Lussac - Paris 5e
Tél. : (MED) 633-61-65
LEFOR OPENO
ZAKOPANE
Altitude : 1000 - 2000 m. POLOGNE
BREUIL CERVINIA
Altitude : 2050 m. ITALIE
SAUZE D'OULX
Altitude : 1.500 - 2.700 m. ITALIE
LEYSIN
Altitude : 1.300 - 2.200 m. SUISSE
GRACHEN
Altitude : 1.617 - 2.600 m. SUISSE
ISCHGL
Altitude : 1375 - 2.350 m. AUTRICHE
VARS
HAUTES-ALPES
Altitude : 1.850 - 2.700 m. FRANCE
SAINT-VERAN-MOLINES
HAUTES-ALPES
Altitude : 1.800 - 2.700 m. FRANCE
LA MOLINA
Altitude : 1.700 - 2.600 m. ESPAGNE
Imp. Desmarye Paris

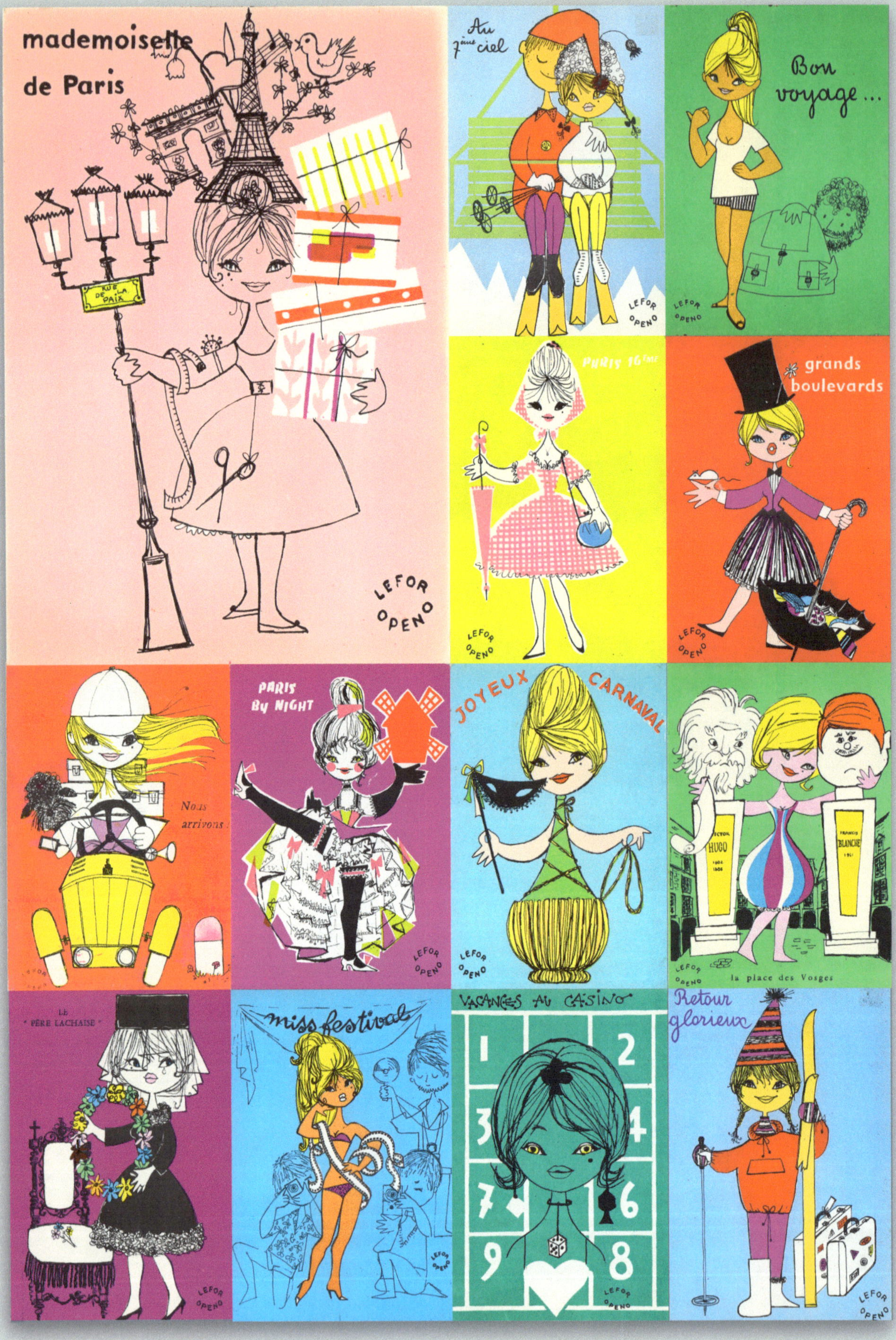

mademoiselle de Paris
RUE DE LA PAIX
LEFOR OPENO
Au 7ème ciel
LEFOR OPENO
Bon voyage...
LEFOR OPENO
PARIS 16ème
LEFOR OPENO
grands boulevards
LEFOR OPENO
Nous arrivons
PARIS BY NIGHT
LEFOR OPENO
JOYEUX CARNAVAL
LEFOR OPENO
HUGO
BLANCHE
la place des Vosges
LEFOR OPENO
LE "PÈRE LACHAISE"
LEFOR OPENO
miss festival
LEFOR OPENO
VACANCES AU CASINO
1
2
3
4
7
6
9
8
LEFOR OPENO
Retour glorieux
LEFOR OPENO

Postcards, 1961

Lefor-Openo (Marie-Claire Lefort, 1931–1971, and Marie-Francine Oppeneau, 1931–2023)
Private Collection, NYC

- By the early 1960s, Lefor-Openo's designs had taken a decidedly Pop-infused turn, showing more young, modern couples and fun, flirty women participating in cheeky scenarios to sell a mood.
- Their illustrations were so popular that they began creating commercial products ranging from postcards to housewares, each featuring their signature spunky female protagonist.
- These are just a few samples of dozens of postcards produced by Lefor-Openo in the 1960s. Some reference famous French landmarks like Père Lachaise Cemetery (the joke being that the word for "chair" in French is "chaise") and the Moulin Rouge cabaret, while others offer standard well-wishes to the recipient.

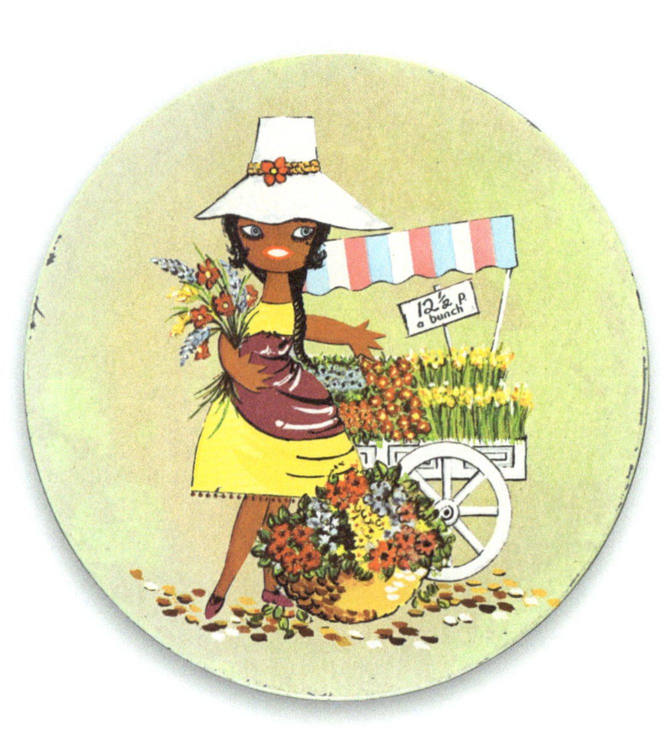

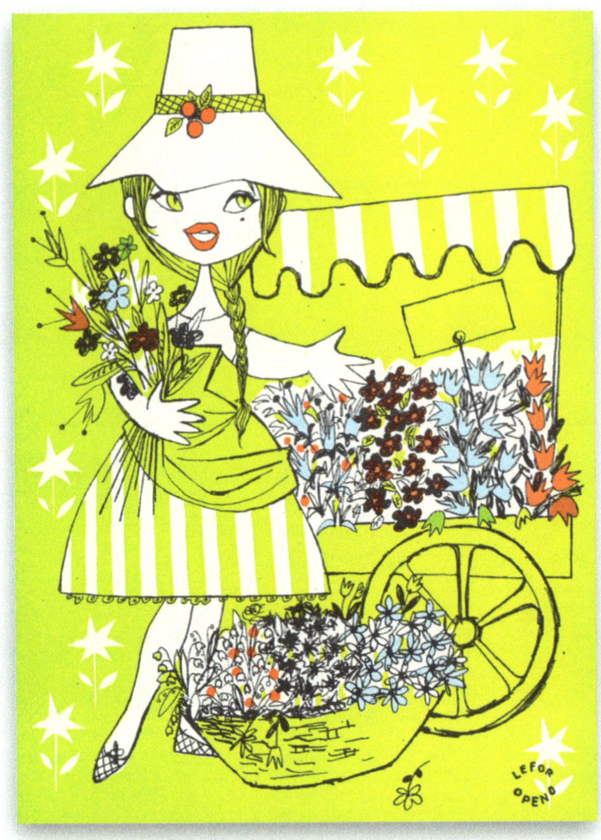

Cookie Tin, c. 1961
Lefor-Openo (Marie-Claire Lefort, 1931–1971, and Marie-Francine Oppeneau, 1931–2023)
Private Collection, NYC

Le Marché Aux Fleurs, c. 1961
Lefor-Openo (Marie-Claire Lefort, 1931–1971, and Marie-Francine Oppeneau, 1931–2023)
Collection of Fionn Halleman, France

- As Lefor-Openo's popularity grew, so did their ability to market their designs to foreign companies. Here, the same concept is reproduced in two different ways: the first as the main embellishment on a British cookie tin, and the second as a decorative print for sale in France.
- In the British version of the design, the patriotic colors of the Union Jack are installed on the awning of the cart, and there is a price tag of two shillings and sixpence for the flowers. The female figure has also been transformed into a young Black woman, with a slightly broader mouth and curlier hair than the one in the postcard.
- It is unlikely that Lefor-Openo designed the other compositional elements of the cookie tin, as they lack their general style.

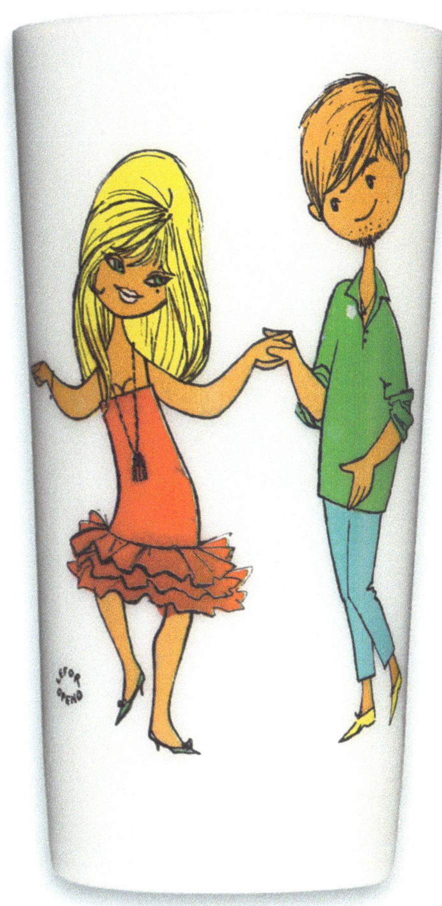

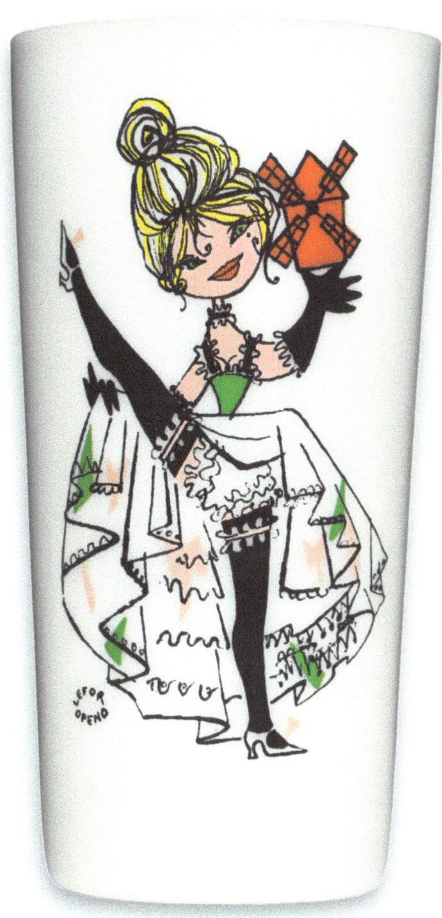

Milk Glasses, c. 1961
Lefor-Openo (Marie-Claire Lefort, 1931–1971, and Marie-Francine Oppeneau, 1931–2023)
Private Collection, NYC

- In the early 1960s, Lefor-Openo also licensed their illustrations to the French porcelain company Halga, which produced a variety of hand-painted objects in the historic region of Limoges, the porcelain capital of France.
- These two cups feature designs that also appeared on trinket trays and postcards; they reflect a national shift in French porcelain production that was beginning to suffer due to the introduction of plastics and other less expensive and more durable materials. In order to appeal to a younger market, manufacturers like Halga licensed imagery from popular designers, updating a traditional product for a new generation.

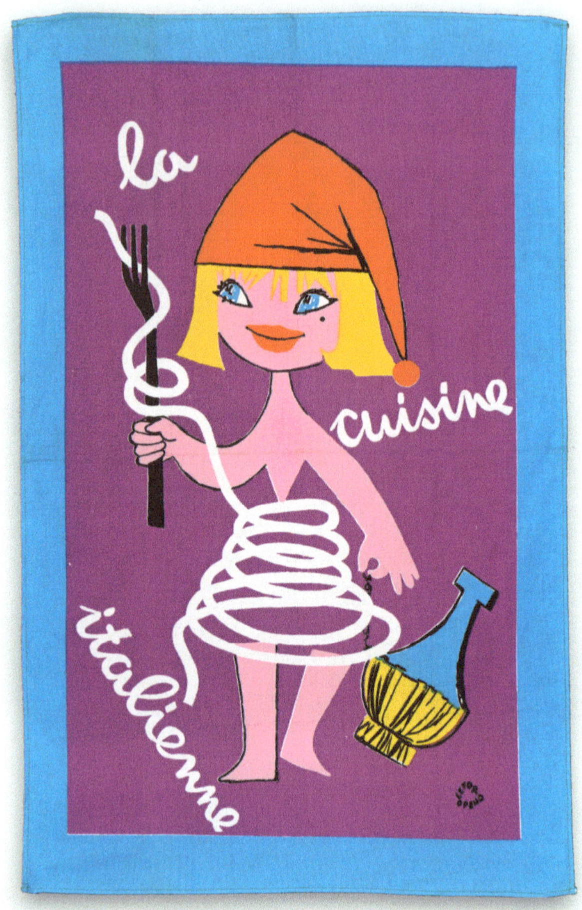

La Cuisine Italienne Towel, c. 1961
Lefor-Openo (Marie-Claire Lefort, 1931–1971, and Marie-Francine Oppeneau, 1931–2023)
Private Collection, NYC

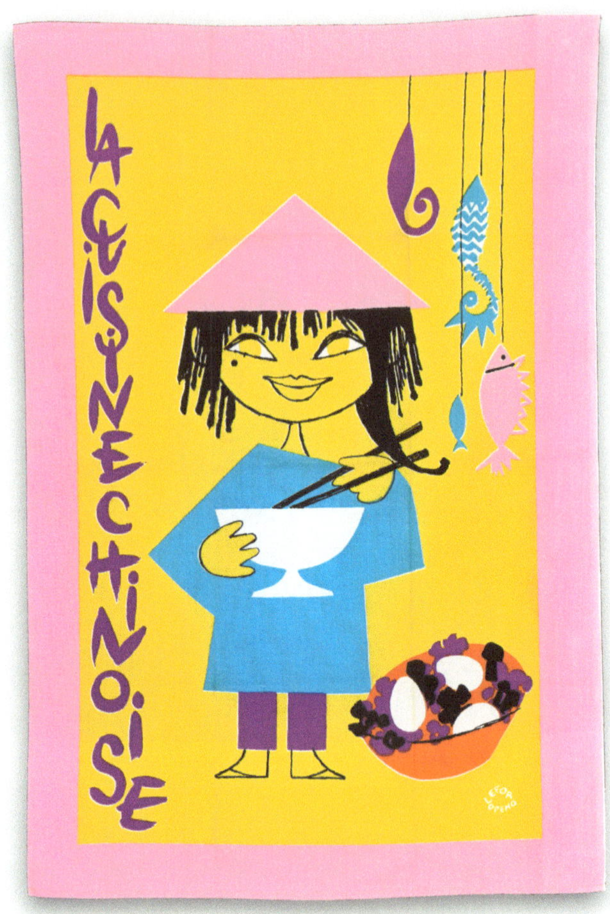

La Cuisine Chinoise Towel, c. 1961
Lefor-Openo (Marie-Claire Lefort, 1931–1971, and Marie-Francine Oppeneau, 1931–2023)
Private Collection, NYC

- Like the nearby porcelain cups, these tea towels were produced to appeal to a younger generation of consumers who were eager to make their homes appear more modern, fun, and worldly.
- As kitchens became more technologically sophisticated, home chefs began experimenting with foreign cuisines. In France, that would have included both the Italian and the Chinese foods referenced on these towels.
- A third towel exists in the series, promoting the food of the African continent—most likely a reflection of the influx of West African immigrants into France and the growing familiarity with the foods of the region among young people.

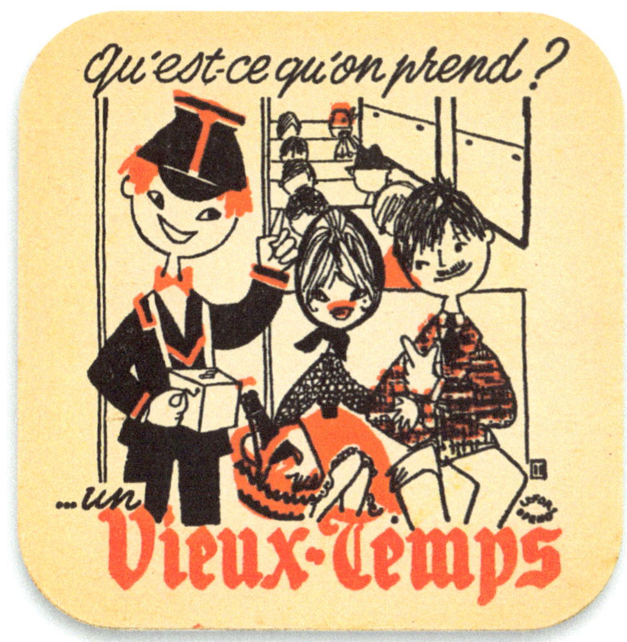

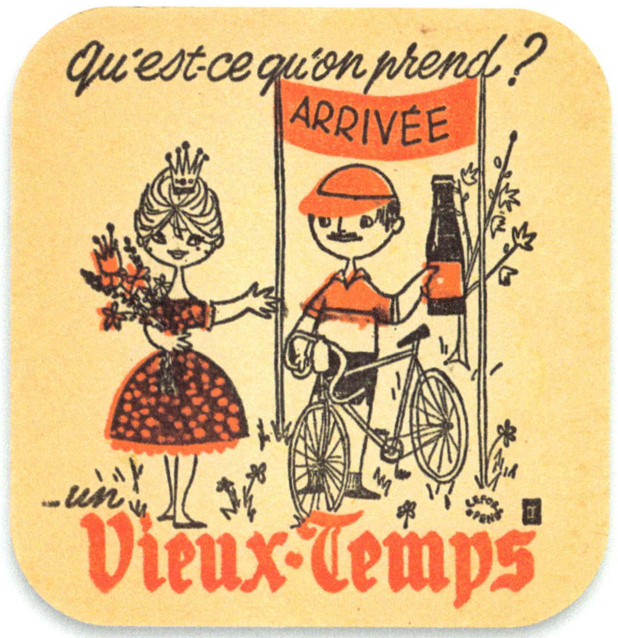

Vieux-Temps Coasters, 1964
Lefor-Openo (Marie-Claire Lefort, 1931–1971, and Marie-Francine Oppeneau, 1931–2023)
Private Collection, NYC

- Vieux-Temps (Old Times) is a light, amber Belgian beer sold throughout France. These are two of many coasters designed by Lefor-Openo for the brand and would have been used in bars around the country. Each asks the question, "What are we ordering?"—the answer being "Vieux-Temps."
- Both examples highlight young couples preparing for a romantic afternoon or evening, a theme often addressed in French advertising of the period and one that also relates to the cultural preoccupation with marriage.
- The choice of a bicycle race as one of the motifs for a coaster is also a likely reference to the famous Franco-Belgian rivalry during the Tour de France—a competition that was also fought out between the two countries in the beer market.

Valentine, c. 1959

Lefor-Openo (Marie-Claire Lefort, 1931–1971, and Marie-Francine Oppeneau, 1931–2023)

Collection of Pascal Di Pietro Martinelli

- In the mid-1950s, an illustrator named Raymond Peynet gained widespread popularity when his "lovers" were transformed into latex dolls for the French market. His success created a demand for other well-known illustrators, including Lefor-Openo, to design similar dolls based on their own characters.
- Produced before Barbie was introduced to the European market, latex dolls like these were cheap to manufacture and made entirely in France. This material, however, also made them difficult to preserve, and surviving examples are exceptionally rare.
- While Lefor-Openo had worked for a handful of doll manufacturers—most notably Bella, Prisunic, and Punch—creating the decorative boxes for dolls, those toys were still old-fashioned despite the modern aesthetic of the packaging. This doll, however, is a three-dimensional expression of their signature character, complete with a beauty mark under her eye. She was named Valentine in honor of the holiday and was marketed as an ideal romantic gift for a girlfriend (a strategy used in a lot of advertising from the period, one reflecting the cultural preoccupation with creating young couples and infantilizing adult women).
- The pair also produced magazine advertising for the Jamila doll, a series of North African female dolls in traditional attire intended for the Algerian, Moroccan, and Tunisian diaspora.

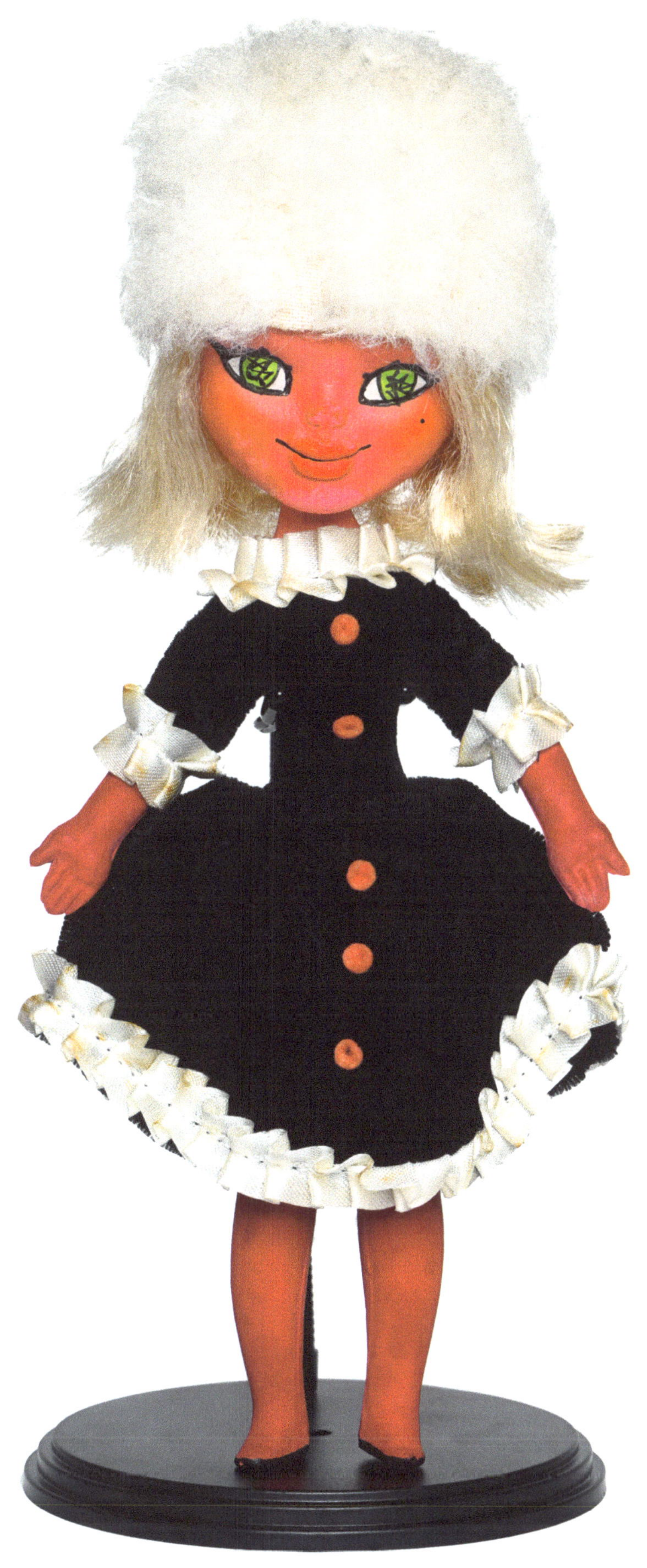

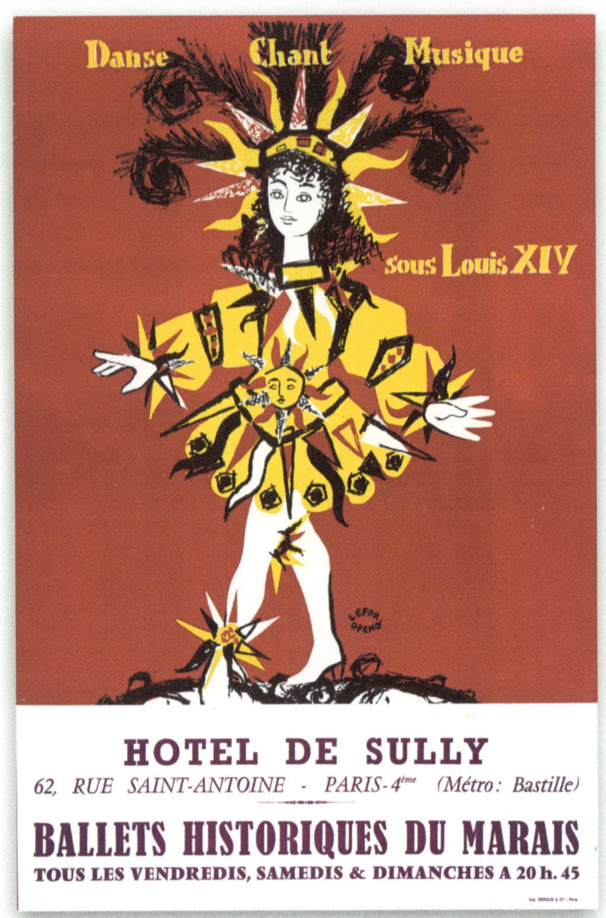

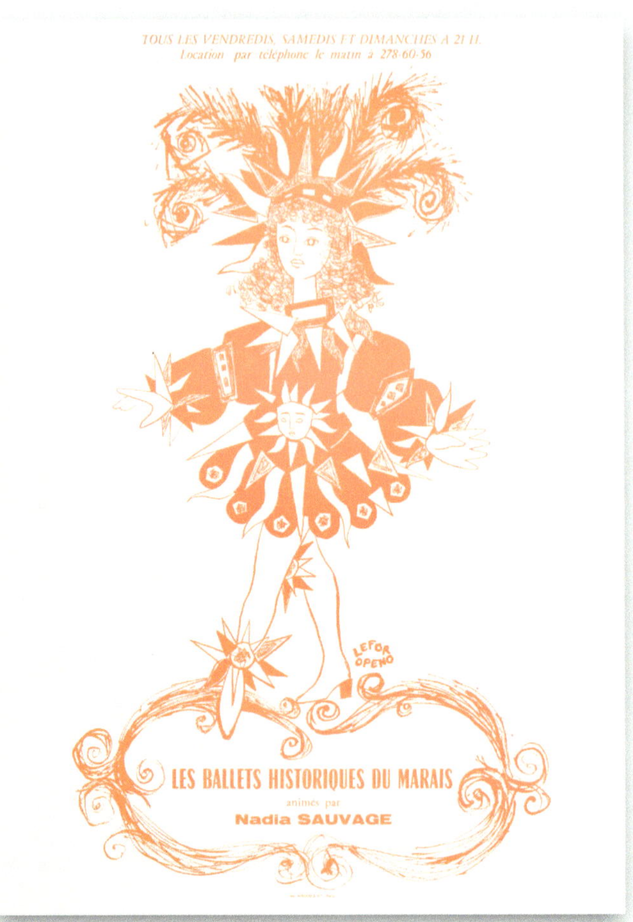

Ballets Historiques du Marais, c. 1967
Lefor-Openo (Marie-Claire Lefort, 1931–1971, and Marie-Francine Oppeneau, 1931–2023)
Poster House Permanent Collection

Les Ballets Historiques du Marais, c. 1967
Lefor-Openo (Marie-Claire Lefort, 1931–1971, and Marie-Francine Oppeneau, 1931–2023)
Poster House Permanent Collection

- These two posters feature variations of the same design used to promote a traveling ballet troupe led by Nadia Sauvage; it specialized in the historic dances of the royal court of Louis XIV, known as the Sun King. Here, Lefor-Openo incorporated such celestial symbolism into the costume of the central figure in addition to other lavish period details.
- Part of de Gaulle's vision for the future of France was the building of a strong national identity around its rich history. Figures like Louis XIV were often celebrated in popular culture as symbols of a shared greatness. Performances such as the ones advertised in these posters contributed to that kind of mythology and reinforced a sense of cultural unity among French citizens.

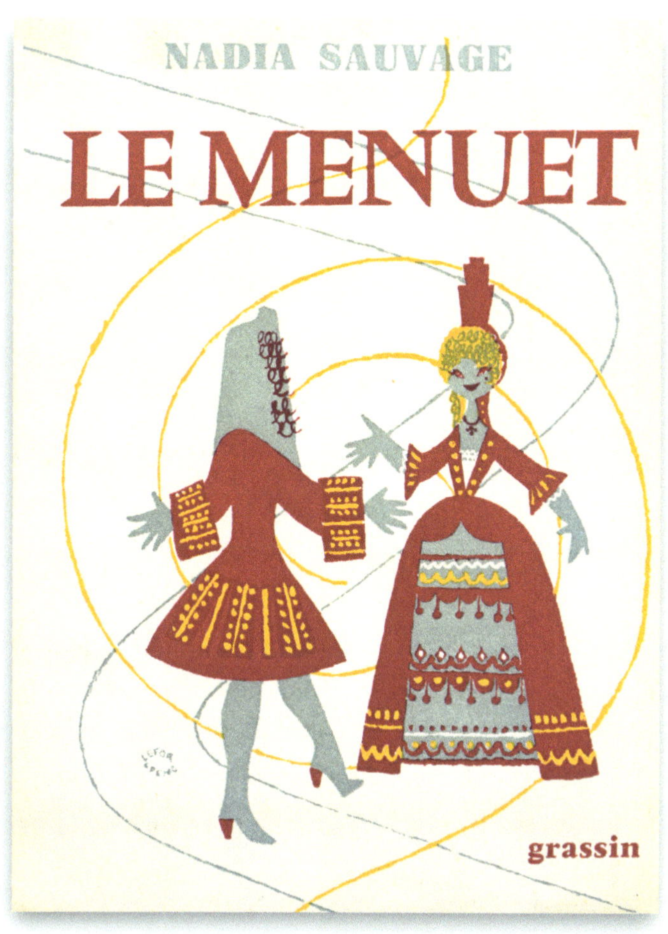

Le Menuet, 1960
Lefor-Openo (Marie-Claire Lefort, 1931–1971, and Marie-Francine Oppeneau, 1931–2023)
Private Collection, NYC

- Printed years before Nadia Sauvage commissioned Lefor-Openo to create posters for her troupe, this book provides a step-by-step guide to the many dances of Louis XIV's royal court.

Milliat Frères Circus, 1957

Lefor-Openo (Marie-Claire Lefort, 1931–1971, and Marie-Francine Oppeneau, 1931–2023)

Poster House Permanent Collection

- In the 1950s, in order to encourage repeat customers, many companies began offering free gifts with purchase or some sort of reward for collecting enough receipts or vouchers for a given product. In France, these types of incentives emerged at the same time as an increase in middle-class consumption. As a result of the depreciated real value of the French franc, buying from domestic companies (like the one advertised in this poster) was also essential, as imported goods were simply too expensive for most French citizens.
- This double-sided poster would have been displayed in a store window or inserted into a newspaper and was aimed at children, offering free tickets to the circus if they collected 10 vouchers from packages of Milliat Frères pasta.
- Created during Lefor-Openo's early period, the message of the design highlights the growing consumer culture in France and the new advertising techniques used to encourage it.

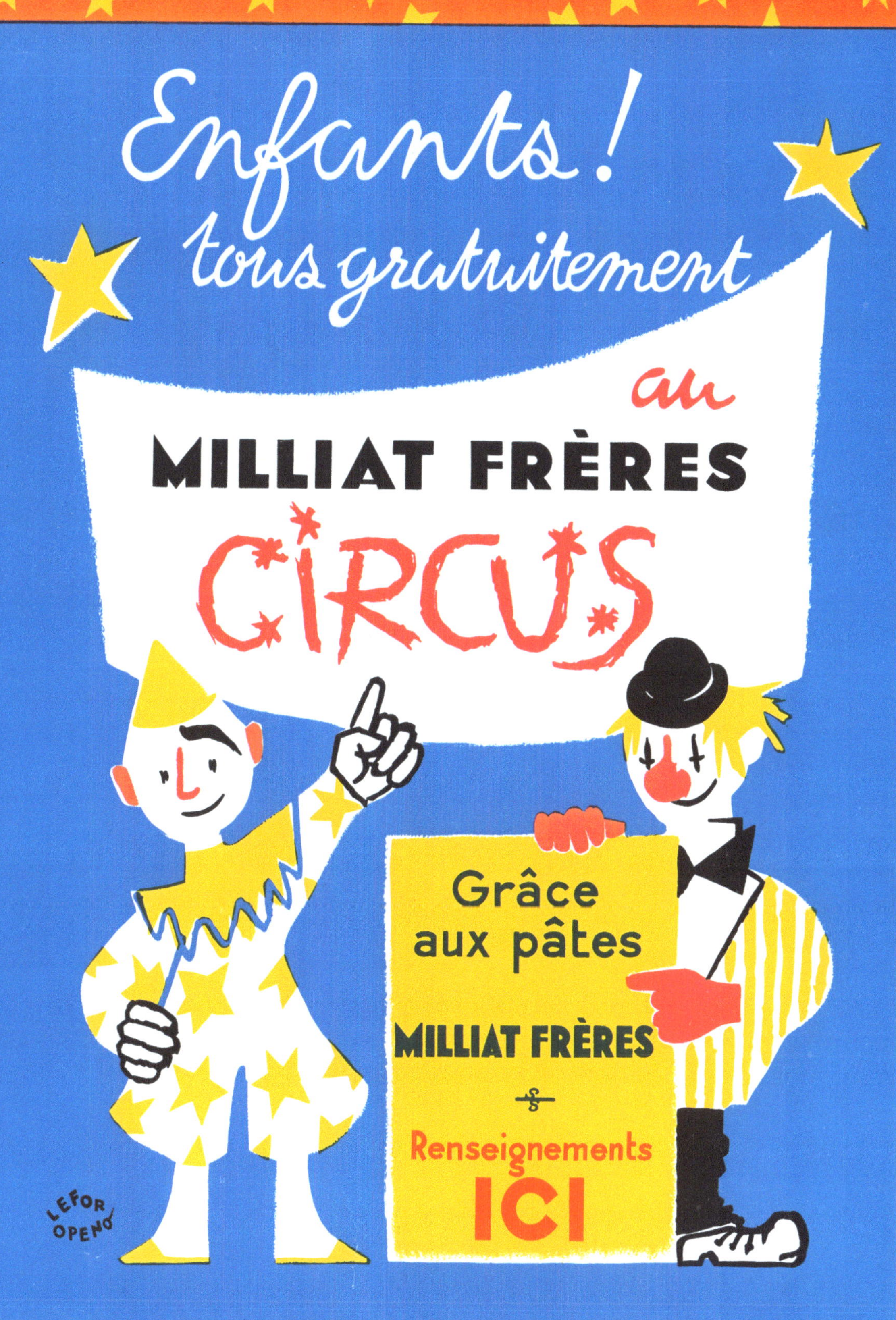
Enfants !
tous gratuitement
au
MILLIAT FRÈRES
CIRCUS
Grâce
aux pâtes
MILLIAT FRÈRES
Renseignements
ICI
LEFOR
OPENO
DUFOURNET

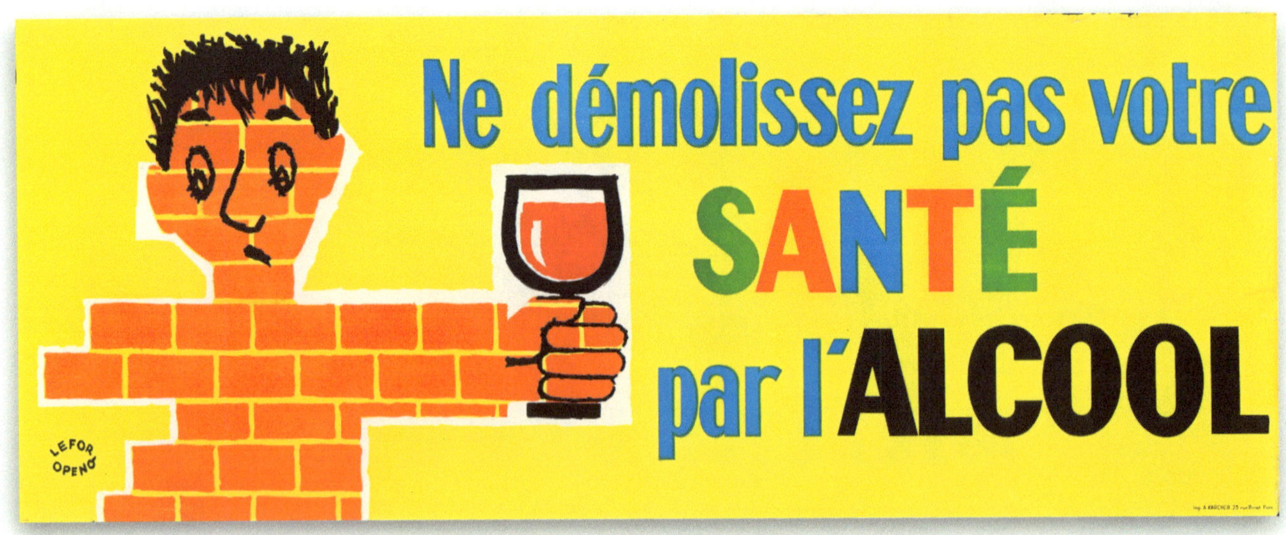

Santé, c. 1956
Lefor-Openo (Marie-Çlaire Lefort, 1931–1971, and Marie-Francine Oppeneau, 1931–2023)
Collection of Fionn Halleman, France

- The high rate of alcohol consumption within France was a concern for the government. In the workplace, it contributed to accidents as well as a decline in productivity. Within society, it often led to domestic abuse, neglect, and other moral issues that resulted in public shame. To counter this, in 1955 the government launched the Health-Sobriety campaign, commissioning dozens of different poster designers to create visually arresting images that would stay in viewers' minds.
- The first posters appeared on buses and subway stations in Paris, but they quickly spread to commuter roads and railway routes extending out from the capital. By 1956, more than 500 billboards were dedicated to consistently promoting the campaign.
- Lefor-Openo's poster is one of the best known from the period and features a young man made of bricks who is slowly eroding. Beside him, the tagline reads "Don't destroy your health with alcohol."

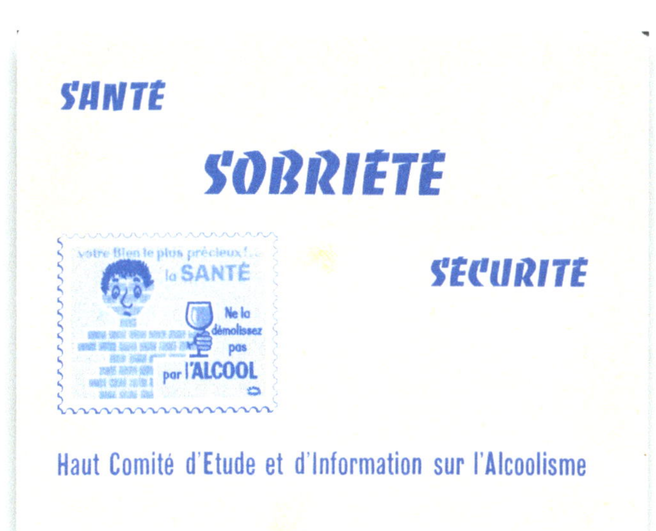

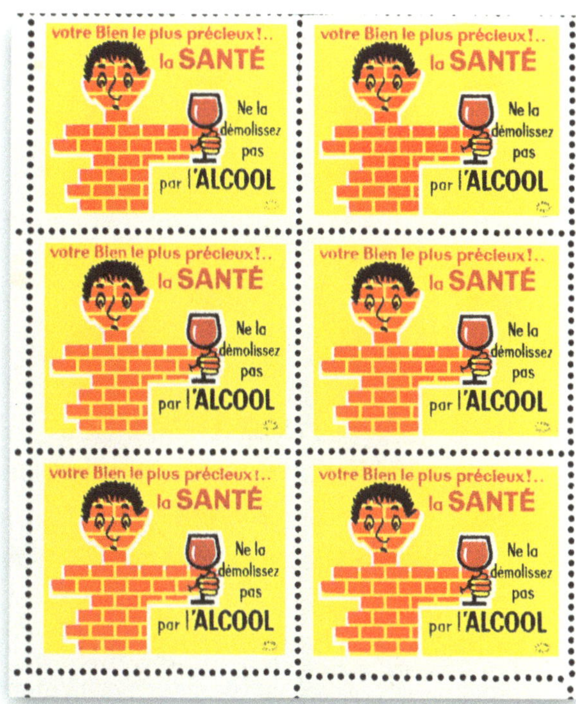

Santé, Sobriété, Sécurité Booklet, 1957
Lefor-Openo (Marie-Claire Lefort, 1931–1971, and Marie-Francine Oppeneau, 1931–2023)
Private Collection, NYC

Santé Stamps, 1957
Lefor-Openo (Marie-Claire Lefort, 1931–1971, and Marie-Francine Oppeneau, 1931–2023)
Private Collection, NYC

- This booklet featuring Lefor-Openo's poster was distributed with the accompanying stamps to schoolchildren between the ages of 11 and 14 in Paris and 6 other major cities. The text encourages the students to distribute the stamps to their friends and to use them when sending letters (each featuring the line "the most precious thing—your health").
- The booklet also invites them to participate in a poster and slogan competition for the ongoing Health-Sobriety campaign. Submissions would be judged by some of the leading poster designers of the period, alongside advertising agents and journalists. While there were more than 200 prizes available, just 10 winners would be selected to receive televisions. Lefor-Openo's poster on the cover implies that they were most likely among the judges.

Pas d'Alcool, 1958

Lefor-Openo (Marie-Claire Lefort, 1931–1971, and Marie-Francine Oppeneau, 1931–2023)

Poster House Permanent Collection

- This is one of the winning student designs from the Health-Sobriety poster competition promoted in the nearby booklet. It is based on a drawing by Jeanne Guégan, a student at the Noyal-Pontivy school, and was finessed into a final composition by Lefor-Openo.
- The Health-Sobriety campaign focused on issues of individual health, social hygiene, and family morality, often promoting new scientific data that pointed to the various health complications arising from increased alcohol consumption as well as the propensity for domestic violence.
- In 1956, a year after the campaign began, France outlawed the drinking of alcohol in school for children under the age of 14. Before this legislation, all students had been permitted to bring up to half a liter of wine, beer, or cider to class with them, often mixed with water. Students over the age of 14 could bring alcohol to school until 1981, when it was finally banned.
- This poster attempts to reinforce this new law, reminding the viewer that at school "neither wine, nor fortified beverages; no alcohol for children" was allowed. Culturally, this law was met with some resistance, especially in rural regions, where up to 72 percent of homes still did not have running water—making wine one of the most readily available and shelf-stable options. Many did not view wine as "real" alcohol (as opposed to stronger beverages like cognac).

Supplément au « Pharmacien de France », n° 22, novembre 1958 (4).

apprenons cela
dès l'école...

ni par le vin
ni par les fortifiants
PAS D'ALCOOL
AUX ENFANTS

LEFOR
OPENO

D'APRÈS UN DESSIN DE JEANNE GUEGAN DE L'ÉCOLE DE NOYAL-PONTIVY,
RETENU PAR LE JURY DU CONCOURS SCOLAIRE DE LA SOBRIÉTÉ 1958.

A. KARCHER
23, R. BICHAT, PARIS

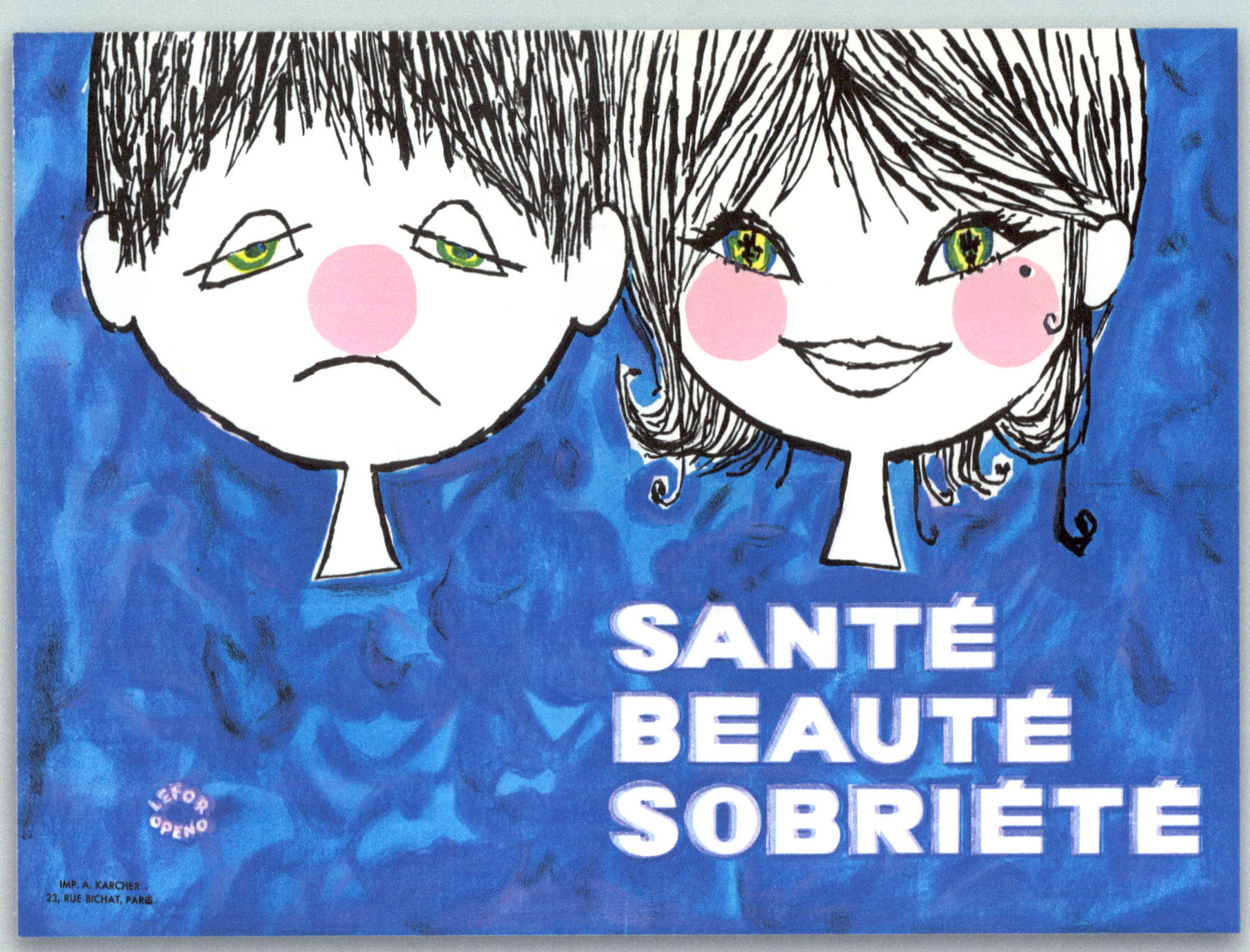
SANTÉ
BEAUTÉ
SOBRIÉTÉ
LEFOR OPENO
IMP. A. KARCHER -
23, RUE BICHAT, PARIS

Santé, Beauté, Sobriété, 1958

Lefor-Openo (Marie-Claire Lefort, 1931–1971, and Marie-Francine Oppeneau, 1931–2023)

Poster House Permanent Collection

- While most of the Health-Sobriety posters were aimed at the general population, this one is intended for female audiences, playing upon their desire to stay pretty as a reason not to drink alcohol.
- The campaign resulted in a notable decrease in alcohol consumption within France; however, the guidelines may appear shocking to contemporary viewers. The recommended amount of alcohol per day was "no more than one litre" (a standard bottle of wine is 0.75 liters).

Fête des Pères, c. 1960

Lefor-Openo (Marie-Claire Lefort, 1931–1971, and Marie-Francine Oppeneau, 1931–2023)
Poster House Permanent Collection

Fête des Mères, 1958

Lefor-Openo (Marie-Claire Lefort, 1931–1971, and Marie-Francine Oppeneau, 1931–2023)
Poster House Permanent Collection

- Father's Day is a relatively new holiday in France, first introduced as a commercial incentive by a lighter company in 1949 before becoming a more nationally recognized event in 1952. Meanwhile, the origins of French Mother's Day date back to 1897 when the National Alliance for the Increase of the Population of France began promoting motherhood and awarded prizes to families with large numbers of children. By 1926, this had evolved into an official holiday, although it mostly honored mothers who had lost sons in combat. The current, more commercial celebration of Mother's Day began in 1950.
- While they do not promote a specific company, these posters encourage material consumption as part of the holidays, with children holding up a gift-wrapped tie and plants alongside instructional language about what to buy as a present. Advertisements like these were printed by trade associations to help stimulate the economy.
- Despite France's postwar economic boom and its increased standard of living, almost all political parties, from the most conservative to the most liberal, were preoccupied with the idea that a declining birth rate was a disaster that would lead to social and financial collapse. This concern led to numerous initiatives and laws that emphasized the importance of family, including the requirement that all children were taught demography (the study of human populations) in school and that their duty was to get married and have multiple offspring. Posters like these were part of a larger cultural and visual program that upheld the family unit as a cornerstone of French society.

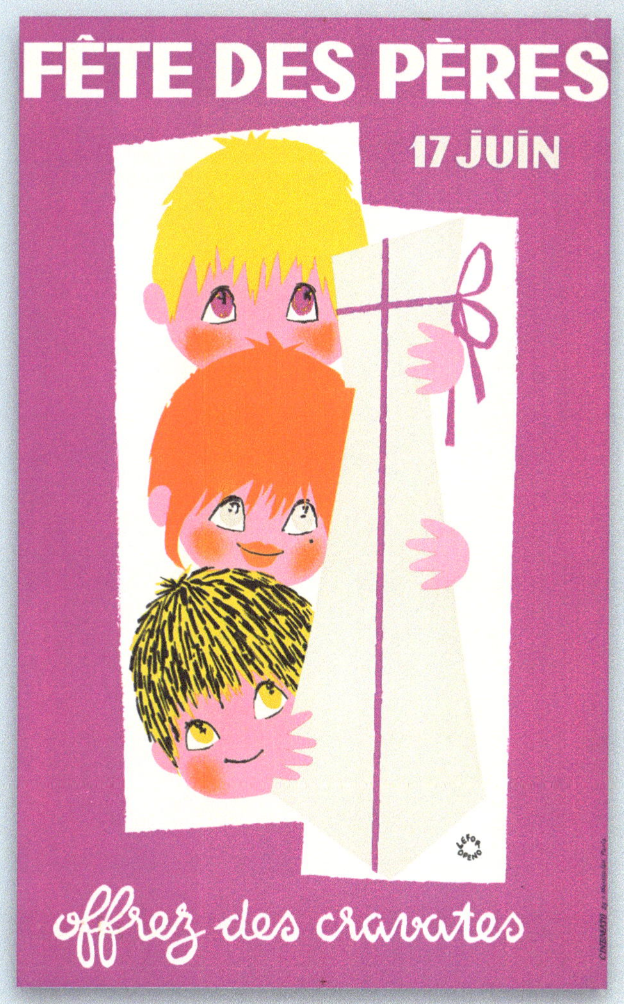
FÊTE DES PÈRES
17 JUIN
offrez des cravates

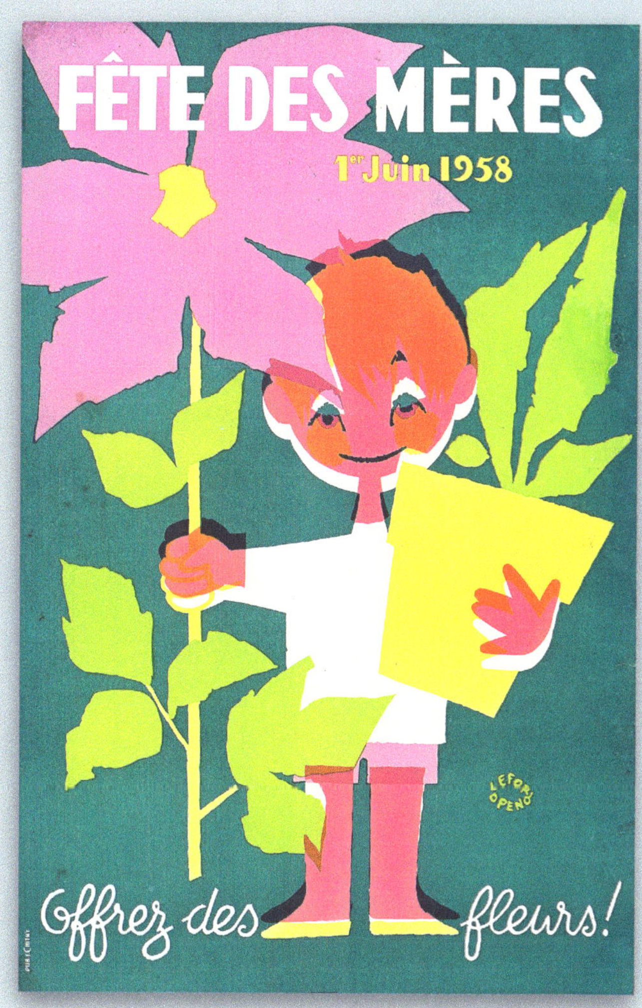
FÊTE DES MÈRES
1er Juin 1958
Offrez des fleurs!

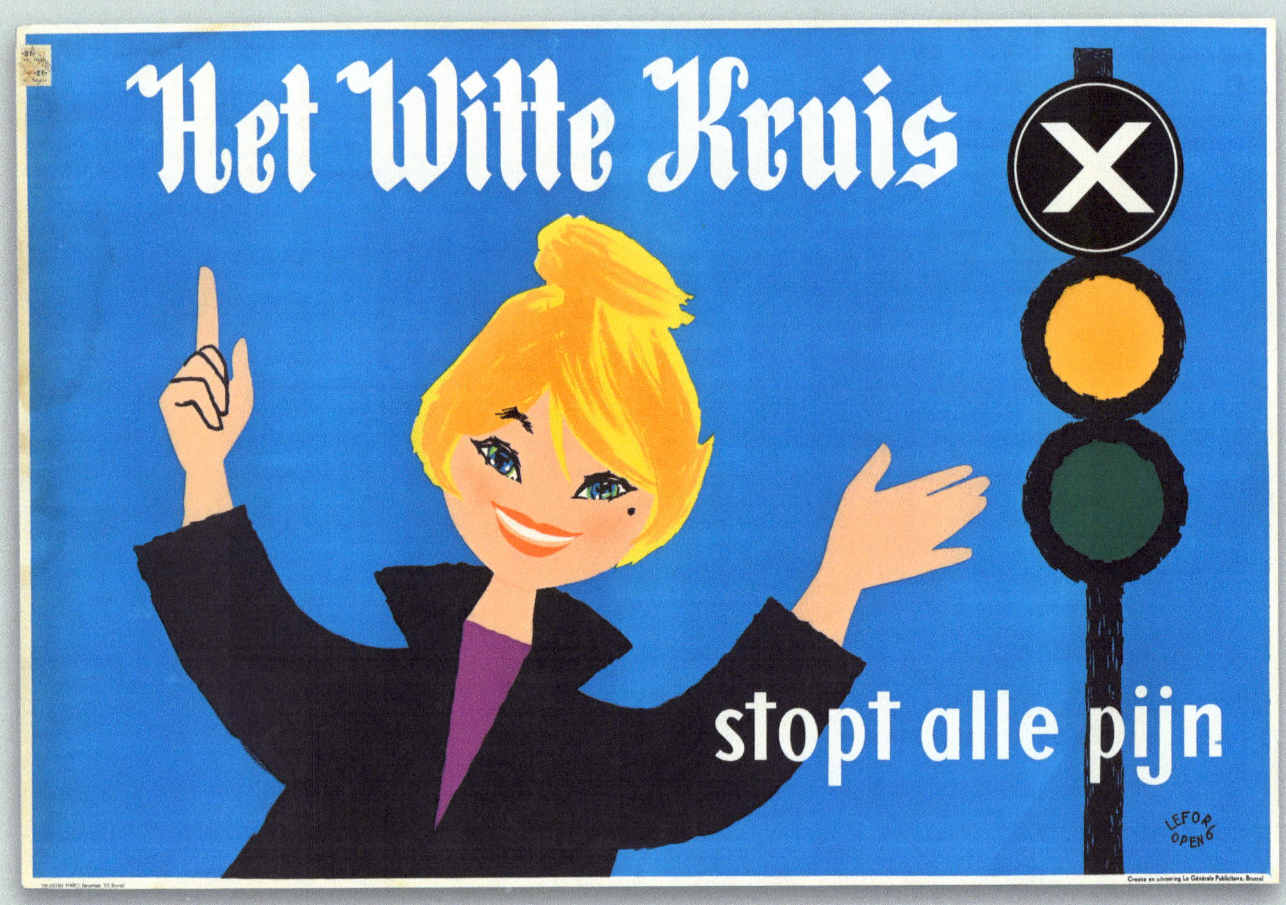
Het Witte Kruis
X
stopt alle pijn
LEFOR OPENO
Creatie en uitvoering La Générale Publicitaire, Brussel

Het Witte Kruis, 1959

Lefor-Openo (Marie-Claire Lefort, 1931–1971, and Marie-Francine Oppeneau, 1931–2023)

Collection of Fionn Halleman, France

- Printed in Brussels, Belgium, this is one of at least three posters created by Lefor-Openo for Witte Kruis, one of the three largest European producers of nerve powders in the 1960s and '70s.
- Advertisements for nerve powders most often targeted women, offering relief from everything from menstrual pain to depression. Available without a prescription, these drugs were often a combination of a painkiller or other anti-inflammatory combined with caffeine and occasionally boosted by a light opioid. Because these products were easily available and promoted as harmless, abuse of and addiction to them was rampant from the 1960s to the 1980s, when the serious health risks they presented were finally disclosed (the most common of which were kidney failure and cancer; in 1980s' Belgium, one in five kidney issues was linked to the overconsumption of nerve powder).
- Although more women were entering the workforce in the late 1950s and '60s and staying employed after getting married, the expectation remained that they would also manage the home, effectively creating a double workday. Nerve powders were promoted as a way for working wives to handle both jobs and were most commonly advertised with smiling, beautiful women, apparently excited about all they could suddenly do.

F06, 1958

Lefor-Openo (Marie-Claire Lefort, 1931–1971, and Marie-Francine Oppeneau, 1931–2023)
My Favorite Poster Shop, Paris

- In the Western world, the 1950s and '60s were a time of tremendous scientific development. In addition to the many time- and money-saving appliances that were becoming commonplace in French households, individual products that solved the general inconveniences of daily life were also introduced to consumers.
- In 1948, Swiss chemist Paul Hermann Müller was awarded the Nobel Prize in Physiology or Medicine for his discovery of DDT as an insecticide that effectively eradicated insect-borne diseases like typhoid and malaria, saving millions of lives.
- The pervasive use of DDT and similar insecticides became increasingly widespread throughout the 1950s. Consumer products like the one advertised in this maquette for a poster were commonplace, encouraging individuals to use them with abandon against mosquitos and other pests. This one even promises a pine scent that is so pleasant, one could spray it directly in their face without any issues.
- In 1962, Rachel Carson's book *Silent Spring* connected DDT to numerous health and environmental problems, starting an avalanche of activism against the chemical. It was banned in the United States in 1972.

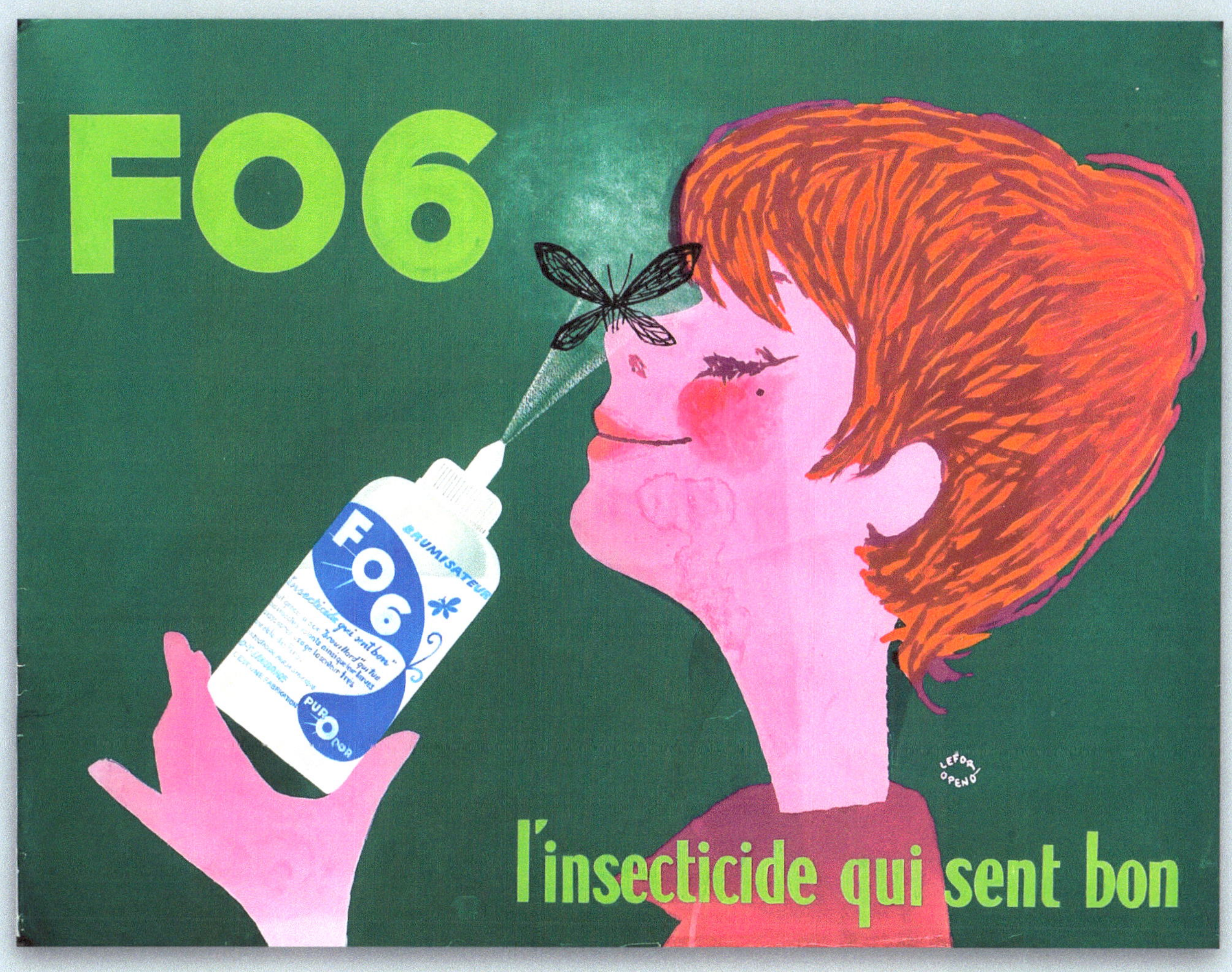
FO6
FO6
BRUMISATEUR
PURODOR
LEFOR OPENO
l'insecticide qui sent bon

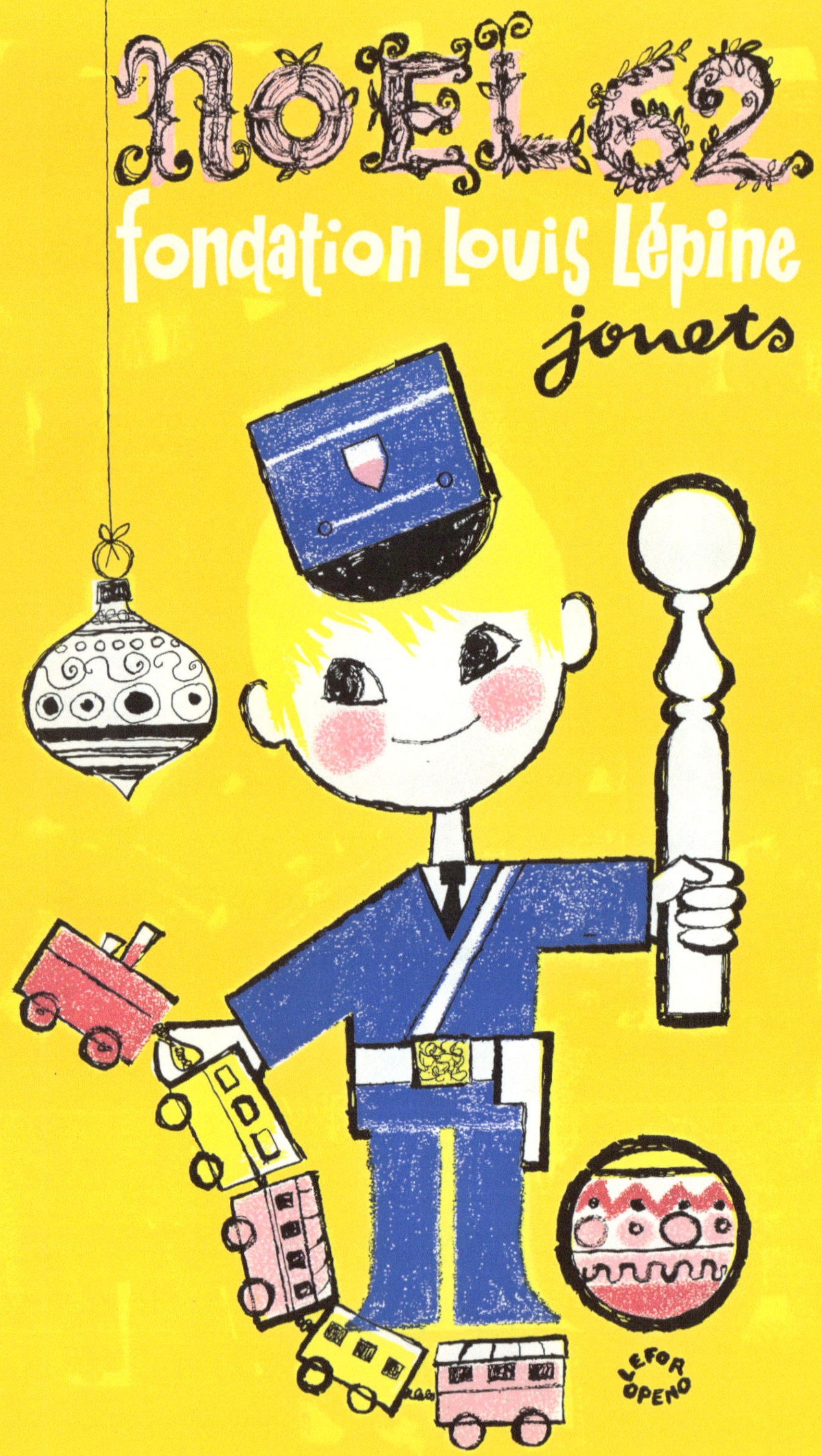

Caserne de la Cité (Cour d'isolement) entrée : 2bis, Quai du Marché Neuf

du 5 Novembre au 24 Décembre

de 9h.30 à 11h.30 – de 13h. à 17h. – *Fermé le lundi matin*

Imprimerie des Services Techniques de la Préfecture de Police.

Noel 62, 1962

Lefor-Openo (Marie-Claire Lefort, 1931–1971, and Marie-Francine Oppeneau, 1931–2023)

Poster House Permanent Collection

- Printed in the lead-up to Christmas, this poster announces an annual toy sale organized by the Foundation Louis Lépine, a charitable organization that supports Paris policemen and their families.
- Lépine had been the governor general of Algeria in the late 1890s as well as the prefect of police in Paris and, like Charles de Gaulle, had a reputation as a leader who provided stability. At this time, however, de Gaulle had a complicated relationship with the police force, with many of his original supporters no longer fully backing him after he failed to retain Algeria as a colony.

Gitanes, 1961

Lefor-Openo (Marie-Claire Lefort, 1931–1971, and Marie-Francine Oppeneau, 1931–2023)

Poster House Permanent Collection

- Founded in 1910, Gitanes is a famous French cigarette brand known for its prolific output of well-designed and striking advertisements. Lefor-Openo were the first women hired by the company to create a poster.
- Gitanes was best known for its harsh, unfiltered cigarettes; however, in 1956, it introduced a filtered version primarily advertised to women. Here, Lefor-Openo reinterpret the company's gypsy mascot ("gitane" means "gypsy") as a contemporary woman, the smoke from the cigarette cleverly forming a hoop earring next to her smiling face. More self-assured and sassy than sensual, she is an aspirational figure for the female consumer, actively subverting the male gaze most often associated with the product.
- Although Simone de Beauvoir's *The Second Sex* was published in 1949 and quickly became one of the most important texts in modern feminist discourse, French society still viewed a woman's role as primarily that of wife and mother. The left viewed women's liberation as bourgeois, while the right typically saw it as a step toward the death of French values. While images like this one may have resonated with young women, they were not a reflection of the general position of women in France at the time.

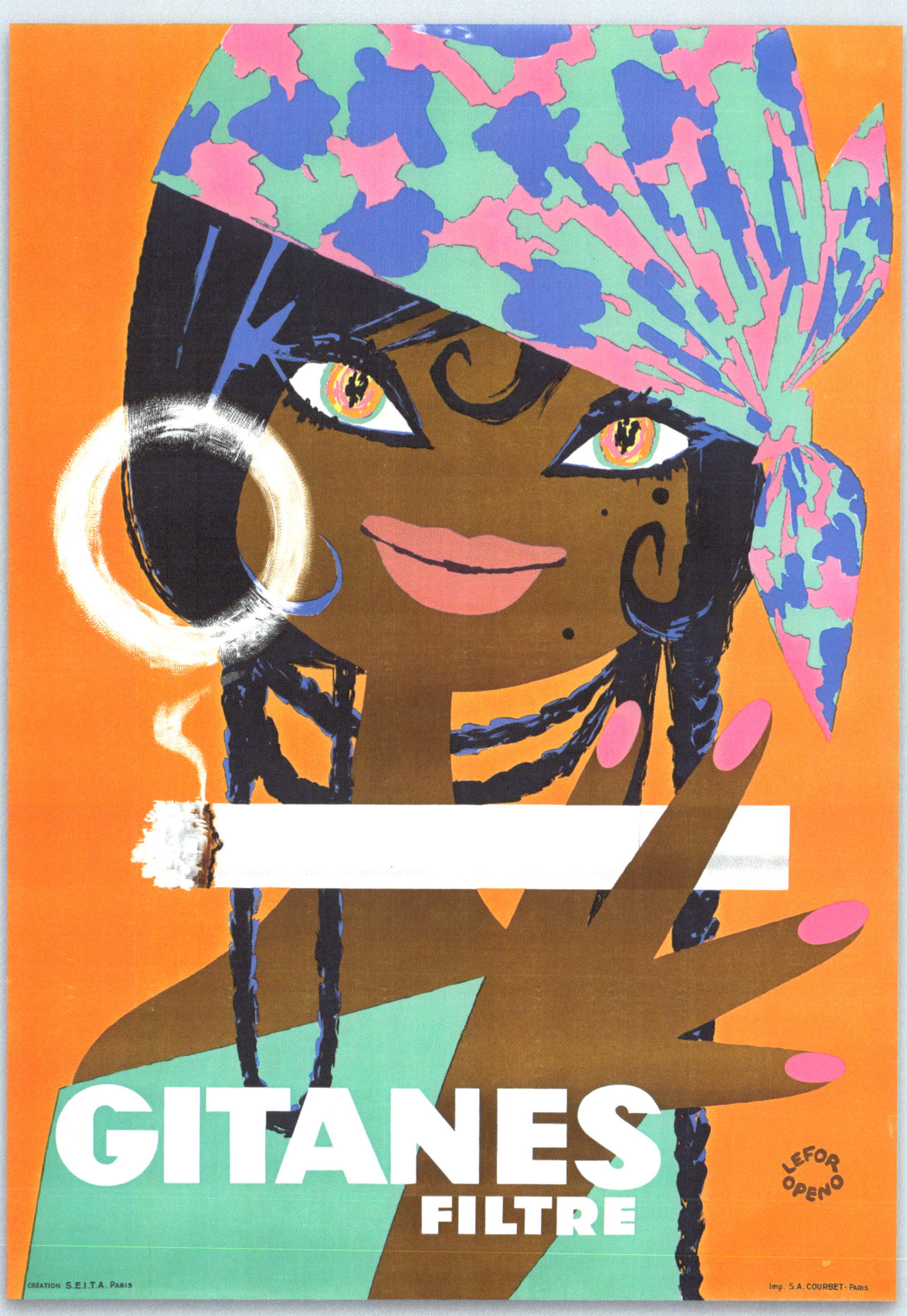

GITANES
FILTRE
LEFOR OPENO
CRÉATION S.E.I.T.A. PARIS
Imp. S.A. COURBET - PARIS

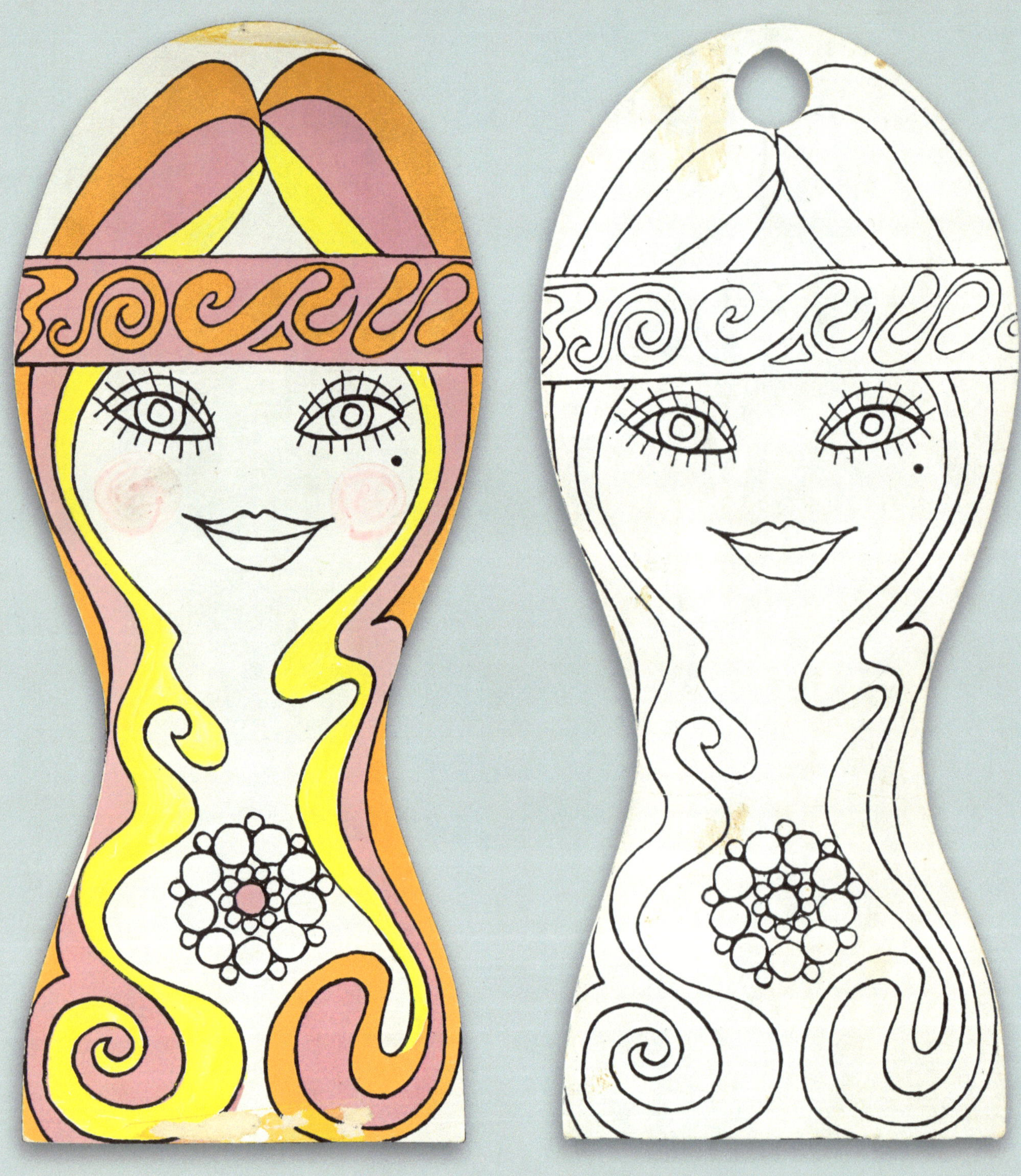

Exhibition Invitation, 1969

Lefor-Openo (Marie-Claire Lefort, 1931–1971, and Marie-Francine Oppeneau, 1931–2023)

Private Collection, NYC

Business Card, c. 1968

Lefor-Openo (Marie-Claire Lefort, 1931–1971, and Marie-Francine Oppeneau, 1931–2023)

Private Collection, NYC

- In 1967, Lefor-Openo moved their studio to Saint-Cloud, a Parisian suburb, where they focused more on design objects than on poster art. The poster medium as a whole was shifting toward photography, and their happy-go-lucky female figure was no longer fashionable. In another year, the riots of May 1968 would dramatically change the political, cultural, and social landscape of France yet again, further distancing the optimism inherent in Lefor-Openo's work from modern youth culture.
- These two objects were produced for Lefor-Openo's new gallery and feature an identical motif—a more directly hippie-inspired version of their signature character. The larger piece is an invitation to an opening party for the artist Pierre Baqué, while the other is either a business card or a sales tag.
- While Marie-Claire Lefort died soon after they opened their gallery, Marie-Francine Oppeneau continued operating it, at different locations, for many decades. She retained the name Lefor-Openo in honor of their partnership until the gallery closed in 2017. She passed away in 2023.

ACKNOWLEDGMENTS

This book would not have been possible without the dedicated help of a few exceptional people. Special thanks are given to Michael Lellouche, Fionn Halleman, Vincent Joigneaux, and Takaharu Inoue for sharing their knowledge around Lefor-Openo and *Les Trente Glorieuses*, allowing us to bring accurate, nuanced information to readers of all backgrounds. Additional thanks go to our editor, Catherine Bindman; our photographer, Robert Feliciano; and Poster House's registrar, Melanie Papathomas, and collections specialist, Alex Stern, for their diligent support in organizing the selected posters.

CONTRIBUTORS

Angelina Lippert is the executive director and curator of Poster House in New York City, the first museum in the United States dedicated to the art and history of the poster. She holds an MA in the art of the Russian Avant-Garde from the Courtauld Institute of Art in London and a BA in theology and art history from Smith College. She is the author of *The Art Deco Poster* and the coauthor of *Wonder City of the World: New York City Travel Posters* and *Art for Art House: The Posters of Peter Strausfeld*. Lippert has contributed essays to *Poster Cult* on the letterpress designer Dafi Kühne, Steve Heller's *The Education of a Design Writer*, and *150 Stories* by the Art Students League. She is a prolific lecturer and was a recipient of the Emily Hall Tremaine Journalism Fellowship for Curators through *Hyperallergic*.

Michael Lellouche is a French author, screenwriter, and former film and jazz journalist. A specialist in the history of the poster, he holds a collection of several thousand militant posters. He is the author of *Protest! Changing the World with Posters 1968–1973* and contributes articles and essays on the subject, including to the magazine *Alternatives Économiques*. In 2018, Lellouche curated the exhibition *Get Up, Stand Up* at the MIMA museum in Brussels. He has also presented lectures on the history of the poster, notably at the Institut National du Patrimoine and the Institut national d'histoire de l'art (INHA).

Vincent Joigneaux was born into the world of printmaking as the son of a printer, growing up surrounded by the scent of ink and the steady cadence of working presses. Immersed from an early age in the language of paper, type, and color, he developed a discerning eye for printed imagery and a lasting passion for the art of the poster. He specializes in French posters of the 1950s and '60s, devoting his expertise to this period of striking visual experimentation and advertising innovation. His focused scholarship and collecting practice reflect a deep appreciation for the craftsmanship, aesthetic boldness, and cultural significance that define this transformative era in modern design history.

COLOPHON

Editor

Anne Cook

Design and Production

Marnie Soom

Typefaces

Acme Gothic

Tablet Gothic

www.ingramcontent.com/pod-product-compliance
Lightning Source LLC
LaVergne TN
LVHW061049110826
845155LV00034B/33
* 9 7 8 1 9 5 6 3 1 3 5 9 8 *